About the Au

Dr Danson Ubebe was born in 1945 and raised by his parents in their country home at Obadan in Benin Province, Nigeria. He studied Science Education at the University of Lagos and took specialist training in Well Egineering at Shell School Ughelli. Danson taught briefly in College and worked at Shell Nigeria for thirty-three years until his retirement in December 2004.

Since 2004 Danson has been receiving inspiration and revelation of mystery of the word of God leading to the writing of Christian books. His previous titles include both *Return to God* (2013) and *The Choice is Yours* (2014) both of which were published with Matador.

In 2014, Danson received two separate awards of Doctorate of Christian Education and of Philosophy in Guardian and Counselling on account of his previous book, *Return to God*.

Currently, Danson is the Chairman of De Ubebe Foundation, a non-government organisation specialising in welfare for the less privileged in addition to the writing of Christian books. Married with Children, he now lives in Port Harcourt.

DR DANSON ENOGIOMWAN UBEBE

VISIONS OF RIGHTEOUSNESS OF GOD

Matador
9 Priory Business Park,
Wistow Road, Kibworth Beauchamp,
Leicestershire. LE8 0RX
Tel: 0116 279 2299
Email: books@troubador.co.uk
Web: www.troubador.co.uk/matador
Twitter: @matadorbooks

ISBN 978 1785891 007

British Library Cataloguing in Publication Data.
A catalogue record for this book is available from the British Library.

Printed and bound in the UK by TJ International, Padstow, Cornwall
Typeset in 12pt Adobe Garamond Pro by Troubador Publishing Ltd, Leicester, UK

Matador is an imprint of Troubador Publishing Ltd

This book has been written to please God the Father.
Every aspect of it is to His glory in the name of Jesus Christ.

It is dedicated to my dear wife, Mrs Mabel Oritsebgubemi Ubebe,
as well as to my parents, Mr and Mrs Peter Thomas Ubebe Ogbomon
– all of blessed memory.

Acknowledgments

The New King James Version of the Holy Bible is a reliable partner and is credited with all the references in this book.

My special thanks to Gilgal University and the African College of Christian Education and Seminary. They have been foremost to recognise the contributions made to the body of Christ and humanity by my published books *Return to God* and *The Choice is Yours*.

Many readers who have made contact with me to testify to the great inspiration and liberation which they derive from reading the books have also been a source of encouragement. I appreciate them.

The place of my wife, Mrs Angela Teigbanyou Ubebe, and our children in the whole effort to write this book is foremost in my heart. I hereby express my gratitude to them all for their unflinching support and encouragement.

Beyond the accolades from readers of my previous books and support from my family is the hunch I received now and then from the Holy Spirit – the only genuine teacher of the truth of the word of God.

So the actual credit for the completion of this work goes to our God the Father, to whom be the glory and honour in the name of Jesus Christ.

Contents

Examination of life after mortal death
Examination of life after birth – choice of life or death

Preface

In a bold attempt to make the works of God appeal to both the old and the young, I received the hunch to do something different from the norm. It is hoped that this book will open a new vista of knowledge and understanding of what the word of God is saying to all classes of readers. It is to meet this objective that illustrations have been provided where it is deemed necessary to make the required impression. It offers the opportunity to have a glimpse of the architecture of creation. This will certainly show that the highest wisdom and knowledge of man is nothing near those of God (Isaiah 55:8–9).

The scope of the book fundamentally tracks the path of grace from Genesis to Revelations. I dare to suggest that no book of this kind, and in this genre, might have been published before now. It offers a wide range of uncommon knowledge and understanding, even in some hitherto comfort zones of perceived truth.

That might be a hard pill to swallow for those who have already been caught in the whirlwind of deceit or untruth.

In this labour of love my choice is to please God, and not any man. So I do not mean any offence by staying outside the dogma of establishments and 'men of God' of repute. The truth must be told by holding fast only to the gospel of Jesus crucified, come rain or sunshine (1 Corinthian 2:2). This is the objective of this book – *Vision of Righteousness of God*.

The book makes a bold attempt to open up on the fate of the Dragon and the beast and his prophet at the end of time. That which is now popularly regarded as the 'rapture' is examined, and properly labelled as the invitation to the marriage of the Lamb of God.

Read it with an open mind. Then you will be better off in working out the salvation of your soul, and in the hope of receiving the prize of the crown of righteousness.

Chapter One

Visions of the Heavens and Earth.

Model architecture of a celestial world outside of time (1 Cor. 15:40)

The is the utmost Heaven where God is
(1Tim. 6:15-16).
His Kingdom rules over all (Ps. 103:19).

Who created God?

Heaven – the angels' abode (Is. 14:13–14; Rev. 1:1b;
12:7–9)
(the Kingdom of Light for angels)

Heaven – the stars above (Gen. 15:5), "sons of God"
(Job 1:6); "morning stars" (Job 38:7)
(The Kingdom of Light for sons and stars)

Earth – created from nothing. It was initially darkness, a metaphor for dead or forgetfullness of God. Out of it God made Celestial kingdom of Light for man to live forever (¹Cor.15:40) and left the best part as night (Gen.1:5a) or dead (Rev. 20:14). It was here God made man another speaking spirit (Gen. 2:7) and put him in Eden (Gen. 2:8). As God stretched out the darkness to form terrestrial earth
(Is. 42:5) to dwell in (Is. 40:22.)

The Heavens and Earth of Truth

1

Stretched out darkness to form shadow of death (Is. 9:2) – the visible world and invisible Air (Ps 23:4a).
Model Architecture of Visible Heaven and earth, subjected to time

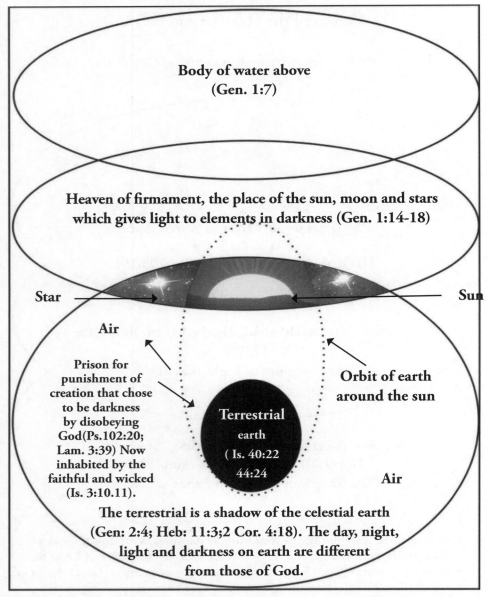

This architecture suggests the remoteness of man from the truth, and the dismal limit of trust in scholarship to understand creation and the Creator (Col. 1:16).. Everything in this world is of darkness and in sin (Eph. 5:8) which separated man from God (Is. 59:2).

Narrative on vision of heavens and earth

Who created God?

History suggests that the word of the Holy Bible is the only infallible testimony that has survived the test of time in human knowledge. It is by it we glimpse into the architecture of creation and know that God alone dwells in the utmost heaven. The scripture reveals Him to be the immortal King of Light and that in Him dwells unapproachable light (1 Tim. 6:16).

This Light is the ultimate source of life (John 1:4).

What this suggests is that without this light, which is embodied in God alone, there cannot be true life anywhere else.

So, unless God reveals knowledge the intellect of man zeros out (1Cor. 2:10-12). This affirms the scripture which has revealed that He is sovereign and that He has been from everlasting, and the giver of true life to all creatures (Psalm 93:2).

It suggests therefore that in the entire design of life, there is no other entity higher than God, or besides Him (Is. 45: 5-7; 46:9-10).

This additionally suggests that God is the self eligible Creator of all things and was Himself not created (Prov. 16:1-4).

The awareness of the name of God is the highest knowledge of the invisible realm that is made known to the intellectual logic of every man in darkness, irrespective of scholarship (Eph. 5:8a).

The lesson here is that man cannot know anything beyond the plain name of God unless it is revealed to him by the Holy Spirit.

This suggests that the lack of knowledge of the truth on the part of the inquisitor often leads skeptics to the endemic question of who created God.

Now we know that God was not created.

The truth always prevails. So seek the truth because it is only the knowledge of the truth that shall make man free (John 8:32).

God of three Persons in One

This God is perpetually in cohesion as the Father and the Son and the Holy Ghost. It suggests that He remains the same yesterday, today and forever without changing (Mal. 3:6).

It is what gives credibility to the declaration by the scripture that Jesus Christ is the same from everlasting to everlasting (Heb. 13:8).

If God is unchangeable and does not diminish what happened to the cohesion when Jesus was on earth in the form of God and man (Phil. 2:6-7)?

What of now that the Holy Spirit of Truth dwells in a Christian (John 14:16-17)?

The answer is that "God in cohesion" remained the same.

Where then does Jesus fit in, as God?

The answer is that Jesus is the **Word of "God in cohesion"** and therefore, this Word is God (John 1:1; Rev. 19:13). The word went out of God's mouth and manifested Himself on earth in form of flesh as per His purpose (Is. 55:11; Tim. 3:16). Hence, Jesus was Lord and eternal of the image of Man in the likeness of Adam of Eden (1 Cor. 15:45.)

It is written that God revealed to Simon BarJonah that Jesus is the 'Son of God'. Then Jesus said to him that 'you are (also) Peter', which means 'piece of rock' (Mt. 16:17-18). This suggests that the Son of God is God and is the Rock and that Peter is a piece of the same rock. Thus Jesus is a full fledge God the Father, God the Son, and God the Holy Ghost, in the form of the Word which comes out of the mouth of God (John 14:10). It is this Word that took the form of bondservant in the likeness of men and in the appearance of a man (Phil. 2:6-8).

This suggests that Peter and Jesus are the image and likeness of the same God. However Peter was created as god short of the full complement of God (Lk.3:38). But Jesus is the personification of the expression of God (Gen. 1:27; 2:7).

This **is the mystery revealed** (Col. 1:26-27).

The Holy Spirit is similarly the examiner of the things of God (1Cor.

2:10) and the giver of the things of Christ Jesus as gifts to man (1Cor. 12:1-13).

By the way all authorities in heaven and on earth have been put in the *custody of Christ (Mt 28:18) who is the wisdom of God for man (1Cor. 1:30).*

It is out of this resource of Christ that the Holy Spirit of Truth takes and gives gifts of diverse nature to man (John 16:13-14).

Thus the holy spirit is the perosnality that searches the things of God and distributes the gifts of God to whom Christ has chosen to give (1 Cor. 12:4, 7.)

Review of architecture – pages one and two

A glimpse at the astonishing architecture of creation is an awe-inspiring mystery.

It is even more beyond belief to find out that God founded the world upon the seas and established it upon the waters (Ps. 24:2).

This idiom suggests that God owns the eternal creation. He proved this by ordering undergrowth and fruit tree to grow out of the earth (Gen. 1:11), et al.

Furthermore, it is profound to read that God alone dwells in the utmost heaven, which nothing can approach. An incredibly high intensity of light dwells in Him, and the heaven is made of the same light (1 Tim. 6:16).

This suggests that God shows His throne only to His servant, to whom He chose to do so (Is. 6:1–3). It is therefore not bizarre that it is God alone that is wise and eternal and knows the hearts of man (2 Chr. 6:30).

The angels of God who do His bidding dwell in the heaven which is immediately below the utmost heaven (Rev. 1:1b).

It was here Lucifer held sway before he rebelled against God.

Below the heaven of angels is the third heaven.

This heaven is the abode of the stars, which God showed to Abraham when He made a promise to him concerning his descendants (Gen. 15:5). It is in this heaven that the sons of God (Job 1:6) and the morning stars perform their calling (Job 38:7). This is believed to be the third heaven which Apostle Paul testified to that someone he knew, possibly his co-labourer (Andronicus or Junia), that he visited (2 Cor. 12:3–4).

The current terrestrial earth was stretched out from the celestial earth before the foundation of the world. This took place long before man was created. It suggests that it is out of this third heaven that the New Jerusalem shall come forth.

Already God has created the new heaven and new city (New Jerusalem) where only righteousness dwells (Is. 65:17; Heb. 11:16). It is now waiting to be revealed at the appointed time. This will be after the current heaven of firmament, the body of water above it and the terrestrial earth have passed away (Rom. 8:18–23; Rev. 21:1).

As soon as they flee into infinity the holy city, New Jerusalem, shall arise out of heaven from God in a manner of a bride for her husband (Is. 52:1–2; Rev. 21:2).

The citizens of the New Jerusalem shall exclusively be the souls that have been saved, having received the complete investiture of righteousness (2 Pet. 3:13). This is the earth that the righteous shall inherit, and where they will dwell for eternity (Ps. 37:29).

The celestial earth is where real substances exist in the form of spirit body. This seems not to be popular, but the knowledge is prime to knowing the true God.

It suggests that it is only this visible earth of matter that most people believe exists.

But this current earth and the hosts are mere shadows or darkness (Heb. 11:3; 2 Cor. 5:1–4). They are passing away (1 Cor. 7:31; 1 John 2:17).

The celestial earth and the hosts exist below the heaven of stars (1 Cor. 15:40).

The architecture of creation, from the utmost heaven down to the celestial earth, is set outside time. So, all the things up to this point live forever. It was in the celestial earth that God made man in the beginning to be another speaking spirit (Gen. 2:7). Then He planted the Garden of Eden and put man in it to tend and to keep (Gen. 2:5, 8, 15). The assignment suggests that God created man for Himself to be the warden over the works of His hands in Eden for His good pleasure (Prov. 16:4; Phil. 2:13).

This implies that God created man like Himself to serve Him (Deut. 10:20).

Hence the man is the lesser god in the likeness of the clay to God, who is the greater authority in the likeness of the potter (Is. 45; 9).

It is in the interest of the clay to please the potter by yielding to him if it is to be shaped into a vessel of honour. The same clay and potter relationship exists between man and God.

Relationship led to fellowship and verse versal and it gave birth to religion in Eden. Thus religion is the practical deomonstration of allegiance of man, as clay, to the potter who was God in Eden. Adam provided this service by tending the garden. After Adam committed sin in the process of service flipped over to religion of maternal sacrifice by the lesser to the greater Diety on the altar built by man (Ex. 20:24).

But under the gospel of grace, God rekindled light in the dark heart of man to shine light of the knowledge of His glory in the face of Christ for man to behold (2 Cor. 4:6). By it God called man into the fellowship of Christ (1 Cor. 1:9) to be priest to serve Him (1 Rev. 1:5-6). Fellowship made man to abide in Christ (John 15:4) as a kingdom and priest to offer sacrifice of the lips of God (1 Pet. 2:5, 9). Thus, it is grace that enabled man to worship God (1 Cor. 1:5) in the likeness of the service in Eden.

This suggests that God made man for the purpose of pleasing Him through worship which took the form of service in His garden (Gen. 2:15).

The scripture describes the means by which this service or worship is done as pure and undefiled religion (James 1:27).

It is this qualification of '**pure and undefiled religion' which** sets Christianity as a religion apart from all other religions of the world. So Christianity is NOT a relationship. What then is Christianity? Refer to Chapter 19.

Let God be true but every man a liar (Rom. 3:4).

The forgoing suggests that scholarship is limited to a 'to and fro' ability to investigate objects of darkness, lacking the knowledge to ascend to Heaven and to descend to earth by Faith (Gen. 28:12, 16).

Descending results in walking in the spirit (Gal. 5:22-23) and having the virtues of the sermon on the mount of Jesus (Mt. 5:3-11).

The happenings in the beginning
(The formation of man)

In the very onset, God first created the spirit form of heavens and earth and their hosts, none of which is visible. They form the celestial heavens and earth and the substances in them (Is. 44:24), including the heavenly man (Is. 43:1).

Then He stretched out from them the heavens and the terrestrial earth and their corresponding hosts for man of flesh to dwell in (Is. 40:22; 42:5).

The stretched-out architecture is the world of matter, which suggests that every visible thing (*including man*) is a pattern or shadow of its real substance. Thus the true substance is the invisible heavens and earth and their hosts (Heb. 11:3; 2 Cor. 4:18). *This suggests that the celestial earth is the homeland of man.*

The scriptures equally testify to this when they declared that man is a stranger and pilgrim on terrestrial earth (Heb. 11:12–14).

They further affirmed that man is a citizen of heaven (Phil. 3:20). One can therefore see why God promised the Patriarchs a better homeland which they waited patiently for, but never entered (Heb. 11:16).

This suggests that it was in the celestial earth that God created man in His image and likeness, first in the Lord (Gen. 1:27) and next the animation (Gen. 2:7).

These two stages of creation form the genesis of the dual forms of man.

They are known as the inward man, and the outward man. The outward man is made to change into new structure at every realm of life. Then the new form will unite with the inner man at the corresponding realm of life (2Cor. 4:16; 5:1-4).

It further suggests that at creation man was wholly spirit being in "body" and "spirit" and "soul" (1 Thes. 5:23).

This is most compelling to be true in view of the testimony of the scriptures that the outer man shall on the last day change suddenly to the spirit form, and shall become like Christ (1 Cor. 15:51–52; 1 John 3:2).

Chapter Two

The Man Created in the Lord
(the Heavenly being)

At that initial time Adam was a spirit personality made to live forever. This gives credence to the incredible ability of Adam to name and remember all of the creatures in the garden. *This suggests that the Garden of Eden has always been in the invisible earth.*

Adam was initially clothed with the righteousness of God in Eden.

But this earth was prepared ahead as the prison of darkness for those who do evil things (**Ps.102:20).**

There is no scripture to suggest that His righteousness was ever in this stretched out or prepared earth. It simply means that when Adam died and he was cast out of Eden there was a change of his inner and outward parts to enable him live in his new abode of darkness.

In this earth Adam became the prisoner of his conscience (Ps. 79:11) to do punishment for the sins committed (Lam. 3:39).

The sinful Adam was cast out of Eden in the form of wholly spirit, to grope as darkness in the spirit realm of darkness in the first instance (Eph. 5:8a).

God alone knows how long he groped in that realm of the spirit before He remembered His promise to show mercy on him (Gen. 3:15).

Later God changed Adam to human form in a sudden change to dwell in the darkness of terrestrial earth to continue his prison until he was saved (Ps. 102:20).

The unknown time gap of the foregoing events suggests the disparity between Science's and Scripture's accounts of the age of the earth.

Jesus mirrored this mystery of God remembering man to save him when He entered Gadarene. There He met a man whose situation was in the likeness of the spirit realm of darkness. Then Jesus cast out legion of evil spirits from the man and sent him to his friends to proclaim what He has done for his soul (Ps. 66:16).

The salvation of the man from the legion, suggests the transition of the man from the spirit, to human darkness, until he might be saved (Mk. 5:1-20).

What this suggests is the possibility that neither the understanding of the Holy Bible's account of the age of creation, nor the claim of Science might be right after all.

The foregoing new revelation is fortified by the scripture which assured that there will be a reversal of the sudden change of man from human to spirit form on the last Day (1Cor. 15:51-52).

This confirmed that the real life is in the spirit realm and not on the terrestrial earth.

The substance of real life of every creation is in the spirit realm

Jesus Christ alluded to this during His sojourn on earth (Lk. 6:46).

Hence it is suggested that whoever believes, will obey Him to do and say what he sees Him do and say. It was the same way Jesus obeyed the Father (John 5:19).

This is only possible when a man who believes first realizes that he is now to regard himself according to the Spirit and to behave likewise (2Cor. 5:16).

Therefore he is to walk in the spirit as Christ now walks, by obeying the word of God and keeping His commandments (Mal. 1:6; 1John 2:3, 5-6).

In the similar vein the true life of the architecture of God is in the spirit realm.

This is suggested by the eager expectation of the entire creation. She too awaits the manifestation of the sons of God, the saved souls.

This is in hope that she too might be delivered from the current bondage of corruption in this current world into the glorious liberty of the sons of God on the day of the Lord (Rom. 8:20-22).

But before then the current heavens and earth which were stretched out shall have first be wiped out by fervent heat (2Pet. 3:7, 10).

Then in their place shall manifest the promise of God.

This promise is about the new heavens and new earth in which only righteousness dwells (Is. 65:17; 66:22) and (Rev. 21:1).

The new heaven and new earth are discussed further in the last two Chapters.

In the current world of matter the terrestrial earth and the entire air space enveloping it serve as prison of sin.

The Air is the prison for the spirits that were cast down from heaven because of disobedience and the earth the prison for man that was also cast down from his homeland of true life (Ps. 102:20).

Thus the man of darkness does his punishment for his sins on terrestrial earth.

On the other hand, the spirit colony of darkness do the punishment for the sins they have committed in the air (Lam. 3:39).

Satan is the ruler and the father of the inhabitants of both the air and terrestrial earth (2 Cor. 4:4).

However, the Most High God remains the sole sovereignty who doubles as an omnibus for His entire creation (Acts 17:28). This is the only God which has neither beginning nor an end (Ps. 93:2; 45:6).

As it has been seen, the Light of God dwells in Him.

This is the Light of understanding and wisdom, which God who commanded light out of darkness causes to shine in the dark heart of man. Then this Light of God gives the light of knowledge of His glory on the face of Christ Jesus; that he might speak as the oracle of the Most High God (Dan. 5:11–14). It is by this that God called man into the fellowship of Christ (1 Cor. 1:9).

This fellowship is by the spirit. It is different from outward evidence of Christianity represented by producing the fruit of the Spirit and imitating Christ in conduct (Acts 1:26).

This happens when man is under the sole authority of God.

The sins which man committed previously abridged his link to the Light of God. As a result, man fell short of the privilege to speak as an oracle of God.

The foregoing work suggests the low level of knowledge of man of darkness in darkness . It shows that whatever level of scholarship he will ever have will remain minor in the scheme of God.

A1. The soul is the first man whom God created in His image and likeness (Gen. 1:26–27).

Soul has DNA of God by virtue of his creation in His likeness.

This is the man of whom God said: *Let us make man in our image* (Gen. 1:26–27). He was made in the Lord (Eph. 2:10).

This was before God rested and before He formed the man of the dust of the ground (Gen. 2:7).

The soul is the man who disobeyed God and so had to die (Gen. 3:19). It is the only time God appointed for man to die (Gen. 2:17) before judgment (Heb. 9:27). He is not of

this world, like Christ (John 18:36).

This obliged Jesus to sacrifice His soul prepared for sacrifice for sins committed in the past (Is. 53:10). It fulfilled the law that requires life for life (Deut. 19:21).

A2. The spirit is the second man whom God formed within man: the soul (Zech. 12:1b).

This was made as another speaking spirit with own DNA and free will.

This spirit is the lifeline of the soul.

It is by him God feeds the soul with wisdom, knowledge, etc. (Ex. 31:3).

It is the spirit that liaises between the soul and either the Spirit of God (Job 32:8), or spirit of error (Gen. 3:1). It's lamp of the Lord (Prov. 20:27).

So it is by the spirit that outside information gets to the soul (Lk. 22:3–4). This spirit was perverse and so was destroyed to cut-off the body of sin (Rom. 6:6). Hence God created the new Spirit in Christ for man to replace the old. Next is to transform the soul and wash him clean to receive God's knowledge, wisdom and understanding the new spirit will supply (Is. 57:15–16).

Who is this soul?

The soul is grossly misread even by Christians who champion the gospel of salvation by grace. As a result, they regard the soul as some sort of characteristics like emotion, intellect and the like. *Nothing can be so far from the truth.*

What is lacking is the knowledge that it is the soul that God told not to eat the fruit of the tree of the knowledge of good and evil, else he would die (Gen. 2:17). So it was the soul that disobeyed God and died along with the spirit and body. It suggests God put off the light in spirit which is the lamp (Prov. 20:27). Then man's nature turned into darkness, subjecting himself to the authority of Satan.

When Jesus died, the soul alone was not destroyed, but the spirit and body of man were destroyed and new ones created in their place. Rather the soul which God prepared to die for the soul of man that he might be saved was sacrificed (Is. 53:10). The spirit of man was then own by the soul (Zech. 12:1b).

The word of God further makes it known that it is the soul who sins that will die (Ezek 18:20). But he was saved by the soul that God prepared to die in his place. Hence it was the soul that was saved according to scripture (James 1:21).

Indeed, the scripture is full of categorical affirmations that the soul is the principal man, or the real 'you', and not the spirit. God is "I AM THAT I AM".

Thus the soul *is a lesser god and may be described as "I am that I am" to the greater God who is "I AM THAT I AM"* (Ex. 3:14).

The greater God is in the likeness of the potter (Rom. 9:15–24) and the lesser god, the soul, is a vessel in the likeness of clay (Lk. 3:38). The soul is the heavenly man, complete in structure with the essentials of God the Father, God the Son and God the Holy Ghost in a lesser form as god (Gen. 1:26).

In the crucifixion of Jesus together with man who believed, the soul of Jesus was destroyed in place of the soul of man (Is. 53:10). This was to fulfil the principle of soul for soul (Deut. 19:21). Interestingly the soul-man was left intact to be transformed later.

It will be seen in a later chapter that the DNA of God in the soul at creation was supplanted by the DNA of Adam after he turned into darkness (Gen. 5:3). Therefore the soul-man is being transformed by the Holy Spirit to conform to the image of Christ (2 Cor. 3:18). This is to re-establish the DNA of God in the soul and to dump the DNA of Adam after he believed and was born again..

On the other hand, Jesus laid down His spirit of the form of man, which He later picked up after His resurrection (Lk. 23:46). His body died but later was resurrected (Lk. 24:3–6). To fulfil the principle of life for life the spirit and body of man who might believe were destroyed in the crucifixion of Jesus (Rom. 6:6).

As a result, the *new Spirit of Christ was created in holiness and righteousness.* It is this Spirit that God now gives to the man who might believe in Jesus (Gal. 2:20; Eph. 4:24). It suggests restoration of light to the lamp of the Lord (Ps. 119:105).

Similar is the guarantee that the Holy Spirit will give life to the body of man at his resurrection (Rom. 8:11).

It is worthy to realise that the soul has spirit characteristics with a body of the form of spirit (1 Cor. 15:40). In the spirit realm the soul puts on this spirit body (2 Cor. 5:1–4). Now the Spirit of Christ is given to him as his lifeline when he believes in Him. The Spirit is the soul's contact with external sources like the Spirit of God and the spirit of error. It is this Spirit to which Jesus alluded as the everlasting water that He gives (John 4:14). This Spirit is anchored in Christ. Hence, as Christ is now in heaven, so we who believe are in this world (1 John 4:17). This is because the love of God has been poured out in our hearts by the Holy Spirit (Rom. 5:5) and therefore lives by God's word which gives us light (Ps. 119:130).

The foregoing investigation certainly suggests that the 'spirit of man' or the 'new creation spirit' in Christ is NOT the real you, and the soul is the real you. In a similar way, the Spirit of God is *not* God.

In the union of spirit, soul and body (1 Thes 5:23), *the spirit is the lifeline of the soul. It is the spirit that searches and knows the things of spiritual nature.*

The body is the resource to do outward things, which may be directed by the soul (1 Tim. 3:16; 1 Cor. 12:3).

The heart is another name given by the scripture to symbolise the soul (Ezek. 36:26). However, in the soul are organ-like 'spirit feelers' (Eph. 4:23).

This includes the divine heart (Ezek. 36:26), the intellect and the mind (Rom. 12:2), the willpower (Phil. 2:13), emotion which can rule over man if not well controlled (Gen. 4:7), the Mind of God (Ezek. 36:27), and so on.

It therefore suggests that it is a disaster of scholarship to describe the soul as any of them. It is in the same way that it would not be correct to label the body (outward man) as any of the organs, like liver, kidney and so on, that are situated within the body.

It is believed that the rhetoric of: *What will man give in exchange for his soul, Or of what profit is it to a man if he gains the whole world, and loses his own soul?* Is a further affirmation that 'you' are a soul – a piece of God (Mt. 16:26).

The promise by God not to leave the soul in the grave to rot is a testimony of how dear the soul is to Him (Ps. 16:10).

However, the soul which God created in the beginning has gone through some structural changes. First the DNA of God gave way to DNA of man – Adam (Gen. 5:3). Now the soul is being transformed gradually to the DNA of Christ (2 Cor. 3:18).

The status of the soul before the Law of Moses

Until the Law of Moses was given, the soul lived in self-righteousness. In that era he lived by the self-will of his independent spirit of free will. During this period God did not input to man the sins he committed (Rom. 5:13).

It was a period of lewdness when man freely behaved recklessly in ignorance (Acts 17:30). Then he was uninformed of what constitutes sin.

The status of the soul under the Law of Moses

Under the law the spirit switched from freelance to fixation on the Law. *As a result the soul gained the wisdom and knowledge of the law. This brought about the allegiance of the soul to the law. The spirit thus married the soul who is regareded as wife to the Law which is taken as the husband (Rom. 7:55–56).*

But man could not obey the laws as required by God (Acts 15:10). Therefore the law was not profitable to him.

The status of the soul under the gospel of grace

Under grace the old spirit suffered annihilation by the crucifixion of Jesus. Then God created the new Spirit in the Lord Jesus Christ for man (Eph. 2:10).

This new Spirit, which was made in righteousness and holiness, is anchored in Christ (Eph. 4:24). So the Spirit which God now gives to who believes in Jesus feeds the soul with only the wisdom and knowledge and understanding that he receives from the Spirit of God. *This makes the soul obliged to Christ.* It is by this arrangement that the soul is said to be married as a wife to Christ, who then is regarded as the husband (Rom. 7:4). Therefore the soul now lives for Christ, who equally lives in him. But before the Spirit is given to man he lives for himself (Gal. 2:20).

The spirit of man that was crucified

While examining the soul, a lot was said about the spirit of man.

It is observed that the true identity and function of the spirit-man is grossly misunderstood. *This is believed to be the reason for the error of describing the real 'you' as an element of the soul, like emotion; even by 'ministers'.*

The spirit is the gateway to the soul. God formed the spirit with a free will. This enabled him to relate to the Spirit of God, or to any other spirit. This explains the ease with which the Devil, through the serpent, tempted the soul in the Garden by the spirit of the woman. It shows that the spirit did not have the trait of God in him. However, the spirit is the watchdog of the soul-man.

The free-will nature of the original spirit makes him a creation that thinks solely about self preservation and flirts with all manners of spirits. This is the nature that is known as the flesh.

But this flesh degenerated into perverse thinking due to his tie with the Devil. It made the soul vulnerable to ungodly information to live with (1 Cor. 2:11). Flirtation of the spirit with evil spirit delinked him from the spirit of God, making him to lack the knowledge of His ways and provisions (Nah. 2:136). Then the soul began to live a self-righteous life – this was the origin of self-righteousness by man after he ate the fruit.

This was the case in Eden. The flaw of the spirit was a justification for God to destroy him in the crucifixion of Jesus (Rom. 6:6; Col. 2:11), that He might give to the soul-man the new Spirit created in holiness and righteousness (Eph. 4:24).

The new creation Spirit – the new man

The new Spirit was created in holiness and righteousness, and in Christ Jesus, for man (Eph. 4:24). This Spirit is obliged solely to the Spirit of God. As a result, he receives only the knowledge and wisdom and understanding of God. The Spirit conveys this information to in whose image and likeness he has been created who created him and link it to the soul (Col. 3:10).

The new creation Spirit was not made in the image and likeness of God, unlike the soul (Gen. 1:26–27).

When a man has received this new Spirit he becomes the righteousness of God in Christ (2 Cor. 5:21). Then the Spirit will aid the revival of the heart or soul of the contrite man, and begins to equip him by the Holy Spirit with knowledge to act wisely (Is. 57:15d). This further suggests that the life of the soul is in the spirit in the similar manner to how the life of the flesh is in the blood (Lev. 17:11).

It is when the soul and the new creation Spirit are in harmony that the body is used as the instrument of righteousness (Rom. 6:13).

Then the soul-man will earnestly live the life of Christ, Who equally lives in him, and he in the human flesh will live by faith in the Son of God (Gal. 2:20).

Heavenly man: the union of the soul and spirit-man

The pulling together of the soul and spirit forms the heavenly man from above. This is the man who is born of the Spirit and he talks mainly of the things in heaven (John 3:31).

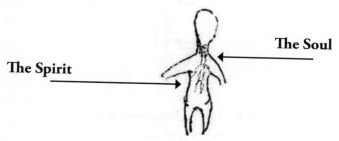

The Spirit

The Soul

This soul-man is 'I am that I am', who was created in the beginning in the likeness of God. The man was made with male and female elements and clothed in glory. He had the capacity to create own desires from what God has created by spoken words of life (Gen. 1:27–28). He moved like God, but was in subjection to Him (1 Cor. 9:27).

As a heavenly man he sets his mind on the things of the Spirit (Rom. 8:5b). But if he lives according to the flesh – the sinful man – he will set his mind on earthly things. This is the situation of every man born on earth until he believes in Jesus (Rom. 8:5a).

This man might either choose to be controlled by God by obeying this word or by the Devil by disobeying the word of God (Jer. 10:23). There is no middle fence foe any man.

The man of the earth
(This is the man of the moist dust of the ground, having neither soul nor spirit))

Clothed in righteousness in the beginning

This is the third man whom God formed. This was after the mist watered the ground. He was made with own DNA. As an earthly man (John 3:31), he is prone to lusting after human things (1 John 2:16–17).

The time difference between when the third man was formed after God had created the heavenly man and rested is unknown. It is this man that forms the animation of the united spirit, soul and body (Gen. 2:7). This suggests that this outward man was formed outside the Lord, which is so. He was not created from God. Rather, he was formed from the moist dust of the ground, which was a previous creation (Gen. 2:6).

The lack of the trait of God in his formation makes him the seed of the union. As a result he can go to sleep (or die) in one realm of life and then wake up in another realm of existence with a new body (1 Cor. 15:36–39). So the man can resurrect from terrestrial to celestial form (Lk. 24: 3, 6), or change from terrestrial to the spirit form in the world of darkness (1 Cor. 15:51–52).

This makes him the mobile temple of the Holy Spirit, which God has built in the last days for those who will believe in Jesus Christ (1 Cor. 6:19).

Union of heavenly and earthly man

Outward man: the earthly body was made to resurrect after mortal death; then assume another body made differently for celestial life – (Lk. 24: 3, 6; 1 Cor. 15:40) Initially clothed in righteousness. This is the frontal for the soul in world.

Inner man (soul): heavenly, created in the Lord in the image and likeness of God (Gen. 1:26–27; Eph. 2:10).

Spirit-man: formed within the inner man (Zech. 12:1b). He is the link of the soul to either Christ or the Devil. He gets wisdom, knowledge and understanding from applicable external source to the soul to function (Job 32:8). This is the frontal for soul in spirit realm.

God breathed the man of the Lord, who is the heavenly man and man from above, into the nostrils of the man of dust, who is the earthly man, to form one complex man in cohesion (Gen. 2:7).

In this way there is the *living soul, who is the heavenly man* and there is the *living being, who is the earthly man.* It is the earthly man that is known as the body.

The union is the origin of the dual nature of man.

So the man is a lesser god, and is in the likeness of clay in the hands of the Greater God, who is in the likeness of potter (Rom. 9:20–23). In theory the union separates out as soul, spirit and body (1 Thes. 5:23).

To identify the principal man, the real you, out of the union appears to be a daunting challenge to man. This is because he lacks the knowledge of the truth and can only know it in part unless it is fully revealed to him (1 Cor. 13:9).

This suggests the error in the popular belief that the spirit is the real you. It would seem that the arrangement of the three in the scripture might have led men to arrive at the said labelling (1 Thes. 5:23). But the scripture makes it obvious in many places that the soul is the principal man, as it has previously be ascertained (1 Cor. 6:20).

The soul is the lesser god whom God made in His image and likeness and called him man (Gen. 1:27). This suggests that the soul who is the image of God is the real identity of 'man' (Luke. 3:38). The soul, like God the Father, is the powerhouse of the cohesion of spirit, soul and body. The soul is fuelled by the knowledge, wisdom and understanding which the spirit gets from the external source with which he makes a covenant. The spirit plays this role of liaison because it him alone that God has equipped for it (1 Cor. 2:11).

It is the spirit that knows the things of man, and it is he who can project out of the union to make a covenant with the spirit of external body. Then the spirit gets wisdom, knowledge and understanding from the external source he chose to deal with. After that he transmits it to the soul to work with. It is this arrangement that determines whether the soul will act either wisely or foolishly. In contrast, the body is the external cover for the heavenly man, and he serves as the instrument of labour in the union of the spirit, soul and body (Rom. 6:13).

Thus, the body and spirit are what the soul (man) use to glory God (1 Cor. 6:19–20). To do this is to exhibit the righteousness of God (Gal. 5:22-23) and jealously guide both against indulging in what will not please God (Gal. 5:19-21).

The marriage options for man

From the time of resurrection of Jesus the number of options open to the spirit to make covenant with or obey increased from two to three. *These are either the Spirit of God, the spirit of Satan, or the law.* To whomever the spirit obeys, the man (soul) becomes a slave (Rom. 6:16). The power that he obeys is his husband. The man who pledges allegiance (soul) is likened to the bride (Rom. 7:5–6). This is the principle of marriage of man to either flesh, law or Jesus.

Complexity

As already shown, the soul is in the body and the spirit is in the soul (1 Thes. 5:23). This suggests that the spirit is in the forefront in the spirit realm in the similar way the body is in the forefront in the material world. In a similar way, man is in Christ and He is in God, just as God is in Christ and He is in man. It is the same principle which is applied in the declaration by the scripture, that man is the head of woman and head of man is Christ, and His head is God (1 Cor. 11:3).

Thus woman is inside man, he is in turn inside Jesus and He is inside God. This suggests why Jesus did not choose any woman as an apostle. So any man who abdicates his headship to his wife to lead flocks might have designed his own scheme and dishonoured God.

Chapter Three

God put Adam in Eden and Formed Eve Later

The Command of God to Adam:

Heaven

God created Adam as another speaking spirit in His image and likeness (Gen. 1:26–27; 2:7).

So He formed an own spirit with free will for him.

Then He planted the Garden of Eden and put Adam there to cultivate and keep it (Gen. 2:15).

God spoke to Adam

However, He instructed him that he may eat of all the trees in Eden, but warned him not to eat of the tree of the knowledge of good and evil, which was in the middle of the garden. And He declared: *The day you shall eat of the fruit you will surely 'die' (Gen. 2:17)*. This suggests that Adam was created to live forever if he kept to obeying God.

Adam was made with the ability to call whatever he needed to appear from what God has formed. He was made to move around like God without being obstructed. Additionally, he didn't need to first toil to get food. He had the legitimate right of dominion over the things in Eden. Indeed, Eden was the celestial kingdom of man. *(Reference Chapter 1, page Two)*

Afterwards God formed every beast of the field and birds of the air, and He brought them to Adam to name, and he did so (Gen. 2:19–20). The ability of Adam to name and remember all the creatures in Eden suggests that he had the memory different from what obtains in today's man. After Adam named all the creatures in Eden, God observed that none of them was good enough to be his companion. So He put Adam into a deep sleep and took a rib out of him. Then He made woman and brought her to Adam to be his mate. Quite impressed, Adam later named the woman Eve (Gen. 2:22–23). This suggests the origin of clinical operation, even though it was done without hand.

It suggests that the first intent of marriage is for the man and woman to become one flesh through companionship: Obey and honour God and have the same mind. This mind is the common bed which must not be defiled by either of the party. Prior to the operation, Adam was equipped to proliferate in the manner of God (Gen. 1:28). This affirmed that there is no marriage in heaven (Mt. 22:30). *It was sin and curse that altered the method of procreation to what it now is (Gen. 3:16).*

Illustration

God Formed Eve from Adam

Hand of god
God put Adam to sleep

God gave the command not to eat the fruit to Adam alone. However, there is every reason to believe that Adam passed the command correctly to Eve.

The scriptural account suggests that both Adam and Eve obeyed the command of God until they allowed a third party to meddle in their affairs. *It is hoped that couples will draw a lesson from this.*

However, God foreknew that man is the flesh of breath which flees steadily from its source (ps. 78:39). So He foreknew that the days of man before he disobeyed Him in the first instance would be 120 years (Gen. 6:3).

Therefore, God preordained the plan to redeem man. This is what salvation by grace accomplished (Eph. 2:8). In the course of the redemption Jesus gave an insight into the frightening, evil nature of the effect of sin. When the time came for Jesus to be the sin which man committed previously, the thought of the weight of sin made Him sweat blood (Lk. 22:44).

Suggestively, it would appear that man has taken the issue of sin for granted and has therefore not learnt any lesson from Jesus.

Chapter Four

War in Heaven – Lucifer Cast Down (Rev. 12:8–9)

God created Lucifer, who was later named Satan, and adorned him with many precious stones and pearls as a seal of perfection (Ezek. 28:12). Besides, he was decorated with beauty; more than in the Garden of Eden (Ezek. 31:8–9). Lucifer was in Eden – possibly for sightseeing (Ezek. 28:13).

God anointed Lucifer the chief cherub and he was made perfect in his ways until iniquity was found in him. Lucifer weakened the nations that existed then and upped his desire to rise to the throne of the Most High God (Is. 14:12–14).

The misdemeanour of Lucifer was rooted in pride, which corrupted his wisdom and defiled his sanctuaries by multitudes of abominations (Ezek. 28:13–19).

The most daring move of Lucifer was his attempt to thwart the pre-planned scheme of God to save man in the future after he might have fallen, which God foreknew was inevitable (Rev. 12:3–4, 7–9). Lucifer drew one third of the heavenly angels to wage war against the angels of God. But the angels of God prevailed.

Then Lucifer was cast out of heaven to earth as Satan, together with the angels who followed him to wage war. Since then Satan, who is also known as the Devil or Dragon, and his cohorts dwell in the air which envelopes the terrestrial earth (Eph. 2:2; 6:12).

Even in his fallen state, the Devil has not relented in his devilish scheme against God. As a result he has instead directed his energy to destroy man and cause him to deny God who created him in His image and likeness to do His will.

So Satan continues to be behind every form of deception, manipulation, evil hunch and desire, and many more sinister plans to ruin the handiworks of God which is man (2 Pet. 2:2). Part of the craftiness of Satan is his ability to change to the angel of light, Just like his angels similarly change to light to deceive man with dubious signs and wonders and speculative divination (2 Cor. 11:14–15).

Illustration of the fall of Lucifer as Satan to earth

Trajectory of the fall of Lucifer and a third of the angels from the heaven of angel

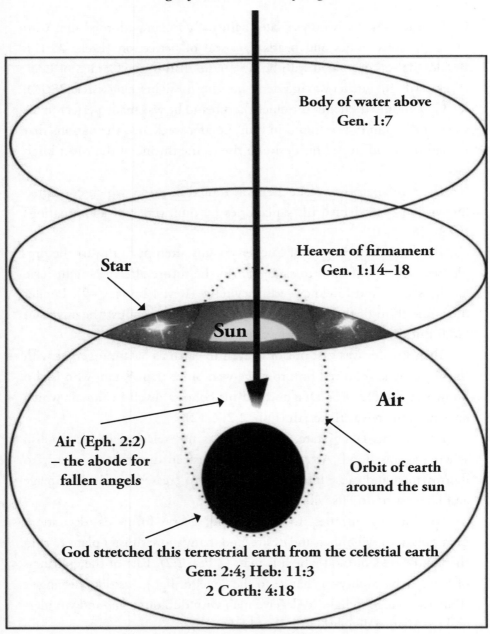

Body of water above
Gen. 1:7

Heaven of firmament
Gen. 1:14–18

Star

Sun

Air

Air (Eph. 2:2)
– the abode for
fallen angels

Orbit of earth
around the sun

God stretched this terrestrial earth from the celestial earth
Gen: 2:4; Heb: 11:3
2 Corth: 4:18

The scripture suggests that there will be self-styled ministers of the gospel of grace who will derive their power in the manner of the angels of the Devil to deceive the people (2Pet. 2:1-3). These are the false prophets that Jesus warned against (Mt. 7:15). They preach a corrupted gospel of grace, and doctrines of men or denominations. To them there is no difference between Old and New Testaments' doctrines. So they preach and teach messages that are unrelated to the gospel of Jesus crucified (2 Cor. 11:13).

In the process the scripture is made to look like an enterprise. Some selected areas of the Old doctrine which deal with material benefit are put in the front burner by the pulpit and made to look sacrosanct in the gospel they preach (Mal. 3:10).

Chapter Five

The Temptation of Adam by the Devil

The serpent (possessed by Satan) asked, "Woman, has God indeed said you shall not eat of every tree of the garden?"

Woman (Eve) "We may eat all except of the fruit of the tree in the middle of the Garden (the tree of knowledge of good and evil. Less you die if you touch or eat." (Gen. 3:5)

The serpent (possessed by Satan) responded, "You will not surely die. God does not want your eyes to be open and be like Him, knowing good and evil." (Gen. 3:5)

So the woman ate the fruit and gave it to Adam to eat. Then their eyes were opened and they knew they were naked. They hid from God. (Gen. 3:6-8.)

Woman (Eve)   **Man (Adam)**

Afterwards God visited the garden and found out that Adam had eaten the forbidden fruit, and so committed sin worthy of death. He lamented thus: "Behold, the man has become like one of Us…" (Gen. 3:22).

What disobedience did to man

It caused Adam to die both spiritually and physically at once.
So man fell from the glory of God to self-righteousness.

Explanation

Ordinarily God hates half-measures and He abhors lukewarm attitudes (Rev. 3:16). This suggests that God would have contradicted His word if indeed Adam only died in the spirit in the beginning. God does not do things by measure. This God has shown in His giving of the Spirit to man (John 6:34).

Let us examine what really happened.

A careful study of the scripture will reveal that Adam died both in the spirit or inward nature and in the outward nature at the same time. Afterwards, he was thrown out in the form of darkness in his inward and outward Parts.

This separated man from both the presence and light of God into Outer darkness where there is total forgetfulness of God. The inner darkness describes the spiritual nature in a similar condition as the Outer experience.

But for over centuries it has been accepted as the true teaching that Adam only died spiritually in the beginning. This has since promoted the belief that the outward form of Adam was intact, and that he lived in that original form for 930 more years afterwards, before his mortal death.

This suggests that man cannot on his own figure out the truth regarding the alienation of man from God.

So whatever error that might be is traceable to the various misreading of the scripture with human wisdom over the years.

Have we really asked, or prayed to the Holy Spirit to reveal to us the mystery of the man whom God created in the beginning?

That knowledge will reveal a range of the consequences of man's alienation from God. The darkness of the sinful man, and his place in the outer darkness, presents a fearful revelation. It will make the most hardened of hearts fear God and hold Him in the highest regard.

In brief, the inner parts (soul and spirit) were made in the Lord (Gen. 1:27). This is the inward man, and he belongs to the kingdom of God (John 3:31a).

On both the terrestrial earth and in the Garden of Eden in the celestial earth, the inner man is hidden in the kingdom of God within the outward man (Lk. 17:21).

God made the mortal (outward) man with the characteristic that he fades out (sleeps) at the end of a particular life span. Then another form of body will emerge in another realm of existence, both having different glory (1 Cor. 15:40).

In the celestial earth the outward Adam was clothed with the glory of God by virtue of His breath into the nostril of the third man in the union (Gen. 2:7).

However, when Adam committed sin and died, the glory departed (Gen. 3:21). The spirit of man was denied access to the Spirit of God at the same time. At one fell swoop, his new world of disobedience became darkness (Eph. 5:8).

This totally excluded the light of God from both the heavenly and earthly Adam. The calamity of darkness and alienation that befell both the inward and outward man together is what symbolises 'to die' in fulfilment of the word of God.

Without the light of God, man cannot see light, but darkness (Ps. 36:9; 1 John 1:5–7). This gives an idea of what this darkness mean in general.

It certainly suggests that Adam died both spiritually and bodily at the same time, knowing that light and darkness do not co-exist.

Then God drove man out of Eden into the earth of darkness, where Satan had earlier been thrown (Gen. 3:23–24). *(Reference Illustration)*

It was in the darkness of this terrestrial earth that Adam lived a further 930 years before his mortal death, as was previously explained. In reality, mortal death means to sleep (John 11:11), therefore Adam slept.

This is corroborated by the prophesied reversal in the future of this sudden change for the man who will be alive on that day of the Lord (1 Cor. 15: 51–52).

On earth man is born into darkness, and he equally dies as darkness into darkness.

But the faithful, like Abraham, Paul and others, now die into paradise to await the day of resurrection. On the day of the Lord He will raise the faithful to receive complete investiture of the righteousness of God in Christ (John 6:40).

Those in darkness are slaves to sin, and Satan is their father and ruler (2 Tim. 2:26; John. 8:34, 44). On earth all are blind in the manner of the blind from birth, whom Jesus used to let us know what blindness of man means (John 9:1–5).

 Adam covered with the glory of God and lived according to the righteousness of God.

 Adam stripped of glory and righteousness of God (Eccl. 7:20).

Adam without sin

* Adam clothed with the honour and glory of God (Ps. 8:5).
* He had a link to the Spirit of God.
* He had a free will of choice to live by his own will, or by the knowledge, wisdom and understanding of God (Prov. 2:6).
* Adam worshipped God as a warden in the Garden of Eden (Is. 54:16).

Sinful Adam

* God removed His glory and crown of honour (Lam.5:16).
* The man's link to God was cut off (Is. 57:16).
* Sin set a wall of separation between man and God, whichJesus removed (Eph. 2:14–15).
* *This death was the only appointed time for man to die once beforejudgment (Heb. 9:27).*
* From day of death onwards he lived according to self-righteousness and was unaware of what is sin.
* But God did not reckon any sins against him (Rom. 5:13).
* God's glory is alien to this earth (1Sam. 4:22)

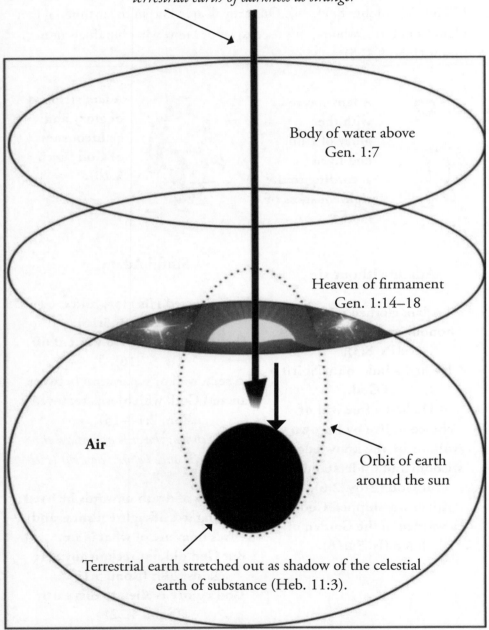

Illustration of the fall of man (Gen 3:23–24)

God cast man out of Eden (his home land) in celestial kingdom on earth to terrestrial earth of darkness as stranger

Body of water above
Gen. 1:7

Heaven of firmament
Gen. 1:14–18

Air

Orbit of earth
around the sun

Terrestrial earth stretched out as shadow of the celestial
earth of substance (Heb. 11:3).

First mystery: change of man and his glory

Adam and Eve
Sudden change from heavenly to earthly glory (1 Cor. 15:40)

As has been previously discussed, the Adam which God created upright in the beginning (Eccl. 7:29) later chose corruption by reason of disobeying God.

The timeless heavens of righteousness detest corruption of any colour. Consequently, Adam was changed in a twinkle of an eye from being clothed with the glory of God to being clothed with the earthly body and its glory (2 Cor. 5:1–4). Then Adam manifested on terrestrial earth in the form of an adult (1 Cor. 1:36–40). This was when he began to multiply through birth by woman to serve the punishment of the curse upon her in Eden (Gen. 3:16). The scripture hinted on this change when it declared that there shall be a reversal of the initial change in the future (1 Cor. 15:51).

With Adam now on terrestrial earth, God occupied him with the work of gathering and collecting earthly things to keep him busy in vain (Eccl. 2:26b).

Adam groped at noonday as a blind man gropes in darkness with baggage of iniquity (Deut. 28:29). Adam was now tare and son of the wicked (Mt. 13:38).

Chapter Six

Death is to Sow the Victim Like Seed, and Birth is the Arrival on Earth of a Wandering Soul in the Spirit Realm of Darkness

The birth of a baby is the arrival on earth of an erstwhile spirit being seeking to find God (Acts 17:27).

Mortal death is equivalent to sleep on earth and the wake up instantly in form of a spirit being in another realm of life (John 11:11). The dying lastly breathes out his spirit man through the mouth.

The dead man and the man who is alive are in spiritual and physical darkness respectively. This is the setting which supports mortal death as sleep and birth as waking. This death is transfer of activities of inner man to another realm of life

Examination of life after death

There is no doubt that it might sound foolish to read that this earth we live on, with all the brightness of the sun, moon and stars, is the darkness of life. This darkness means to be forgetful of God and His way, and to be away from His kingdom. In a similar way, every man born into it is himself darkness, which means that he is away from God and forgetful of Him (Eph. 5:8). The true life is in the light of God.

No man can see or enter the light of God until he is anchored in Jesus (Mt. 15:5). Now that Jesus has saved every man that might believe in Him, all the faithful at mortal death go into the country of paradise (Heb. 11:16), which God has prepared for them to *await for resurrection on the last day* (John 6:40; Rev. 20:5).

Why is this so? Now only the spirit of the faithful has received the investiture of righteousness when he believed. *But the soul and body have not.* It is on the day of the Lord that the soul will seize to require the faith to live. This will be the day he will be redeemed to taste his salvation and put on the complete investiture of righteousness (1 Pet. 1:7–9). Then angels will fish out the faithful all around (1 Thes. 4:15–16; Mt. 24:31) and have the lowly body transformed to conform to the glorious body of Christ (Phil. 3:21; 1 Cor. 15:51–52).

On the other hand, when an unbeliever dies on earth he is received into the darkness of the spirit realm (1 John 3:14b) to await resurrection to condemnation (Dan. 12:2b). The scripture suggests that the opposite waiting places in paradise and in darkness have a common boundary of insurmountable gulf between (Lk. 16:26).

So whether at birth or death, man is confined within the realm that is away from God. *At the death of both the faithful and the unbeliever, the body stays in the grave.*

This suggests a contrast in the timing of the death and resurrection of Jesus, which happened back-to-back with only three days' interval (Lk. 24:7).

The lesson to be learnt here is that both birth and death are moments of change, of dwelling place and of one garment to another, by the heavenly man, where the outward man is in the likeness of a garment (2 Cor. 5:1–7).

It affirms the word of Jesus, which declared that at death, man simply goes to sleep. Afterwards, he awakes in the spirit form with a new attire of the new realm (Mt. 9:24; Mk. 5:39; John 11:11, 14).

The man sowed in sin will wake up in darkness (Lk. 16:23–24).

The man sowed as a believer in Christ will wake up in paradise (Lk. 23:43).

Examination of life after birth – choice of life or death

It has been proved in this book that the death of man in the loins of Adam in Eden (Gen. 2:17) is the first and only fixed time to die before judgment (Heb. 9:27).

In contrast, and apart from examples of the show of power to knock down the defiant man, there is no scripture known to me that shows that God appointed a particular day for each man to die on earth. Such would suggest unrighteousness on the part of God, since mortal death is known to be random. God forbid.

When Adam died, all the souls in his loins began a nomadic life, grouping in darkness (Deut. 30:19). Every soul-man has since been drifting with the intent to seek God, and hope to find Him (Acts 17:27).

It is when the nomadic soul ventures into the radar of the mercy of God that he is born on earth. This suggests that the earth is the territory of opportunity where the wandering soul-man might seek and find God. As previously explained, this soul is darkness and is away from God. So he is naked and dead. It is in this naked and dead form that he is born on earth in sin and iniquity (Ps. 51:5).

The nakedness of man is traceable to the split of man, which God originally conceived as male and female in one body. The nakedness was complete when man disobeyed God in the loins of Adam, and the glory of God which had clothed him departed. It is in this nakedness that everyone (man and woman) is born on earth, and it is in the same way that he or she will return (Eccl. 5:15; Job 1:21).

Once a wandering soul ventures onto the earth, he retains the memory. As a result he will be at liberty to desire to either return or not to return to earth after the mortal death of his earthly body. An example is the prophecy of prophet Malachi concerning the coming of Elijah before the Messiah (Mal. 4:5). Indeed, John the Baptist fulfilled the prophecy before the Messiah (Mt. 17:10–13).

On earth and in death, man is darkness and dead and under sin (Rom. 3:9). This might be the rationale for Jesus to say that the dead should be left alone to bury the dead (Lk. 9:60). It additionally suggests that it is not the mortal death that the scripture refers to when it declared: *And it is appointed for man to die once, but after that the judgment* (Heb. 9:27). Indeed, this quote refers to the first death of Adam in Eden (Gen. 3:6–7).

The judgment to which the declaration refers is that which will take place before the second death on the day of the Lord (Rev. 20:14–15).

Let it be understood that death alienates man from God and that mortal death is sleep because it does not separate man from God in the manner of death in Eden. The death in Eden is the only one that has so far separated man from God. The next one that will separate man from God is the second death. This suggests that the death in Eden is the only one appointed for man to die once before the judgment that will precede the second death. It was to keep man from the second death that God intervened after the first death; that he might be saved to demonstrate His righteousness as the justifier of whoever believed in Jesus, whom He sent to atone for the sins of man (John 3:16). As a result, God forgave and forgot the sins man previously committed (Rom. 3:25).

For every nomadic soul-man who is born in his naked and dead form on earth, God generally gives to him the tasks of gathering and collecting earthly things to keep him busy in vain (Eccl. 2:26). As the soul-man gropes on earth, he will get an opportunity to meet Jesus, the Saviour. Then the soul-man who hears and listens, and believes and obeys Jesus, will be saved from nomadic life by the grace of God (Eph. 2:8). This grace is not a favour to man. Rather, it is the normal working of the Spirit of glory and of God, an expression of the reign of our Lord Jesus (1 Pet. 4:14).

Chapter Seven

The link of God to sinful Adam: the DNA mystery

Adam was created in the image and likeness of God, and therefore according to His DNA. This suggests that the DNA of God was intact when Adam through Eve gave birth to Cain and Abel for the simple reason of linking God to the sinful humanity.

Adam

Cain, the first son

Abel, the second son of Adam. He was the first prophet of the Lord (Lk. 11:50–51)

Certainly God detests sin. But nobody can fault Him or know why He does things that might be outside the understanding of man. This is the mystery of His DNA in sinful Adam. The DNA is indestructible by anybody other than God (Mt. 10:28). However the DNA of God got frozen, so to speak, to raise the DNA of Adam in its place before the birth of Seth, the third son of Adam (Gen. 5:3).

This suggests that the DNA of God remained frozen in Adam in order to preserve it from sinful nature and at the same time keep in view the exiled man (Jer. 29:11). However, God promised not to forsake him (Heb. 13:5) but He stayed away from intervening in his affairs.

Afterwards God accepted the sacrifice of Abel and rejected that of

Cain. Then emotion ruled over Cain due to envy, and he killed Abel. As a result, God cursed Cain.

This suggests that the incident made Cain the epitome of all manner of evil in the world of man, in contrast to Satan in the realm of evil spirits (Gen. 4:11–12).

The self-righteousness has continued till this day. *However, God did not record the works of evil against man during the time of ignorance (Rom. 5:13; Acts 17:30).*

All men are descendants of Adam, and therefore of his own DNA. It is in the DNA that every conceivable deceit and wickedness of the heart is rooted (Jer. 17:9).

Seth, the third son born with the DNA of Adam.

Adam changed into his own DNA.

The first man that Adam through Eve gave birth to in his own DNA was Seth (Gen. 5:3).

By now the relationship between the spirit of man and the Spirit of God has long been severed. Therefore the soul which was in the beginning created upright lost the uprightness, and he began to design own schemes (Eccl. 7:29).

Then man assumed his carnal nature, and he ceased to desire heavenly things. Instead he directed his interest toward earthly things (John 3:31b).

Now the divine heart turned stony or flint, and became impervious to the knowledge and wisdom of God (Zech. 7:12a). The spirit of man became perverse, and prone to fantasise as well as to be tied to ungodly external sources of wisdom and knowledge. This suggests the bond of the soul (the main persona of man) is to be a slave to sin, which is the Devil (2 Tim. 2:26). Then the Devil became the new father of man (John 8:44). This reshaped the life of man to end and perish in the grave (Ps. 49:14).

This suggests that whatever knowledge man might garner in the now DNA of man will not unveil anything concerning God.

It is an indication that man cannot find the origin of life, which is different from the account of the scripture by scholarship.

Chapter Eight

The origin of shrine and Idol worship

The free will which God gave to man made him independent. But it was not profitable to him. The futility of his thoughts and foolish heart led him to disobey God and to believe and obey Satan, which made him a slave to sin (Gen. 3:6–8).

So in a bid to seek and hope to find God, the Devil further deceived man to believe that any image of His creation represented a symbol of Him. Therefore he changed the glory of God into the image made like corruptible man and birds and four-footed animals and creeping things (Rom. 1:21–23).

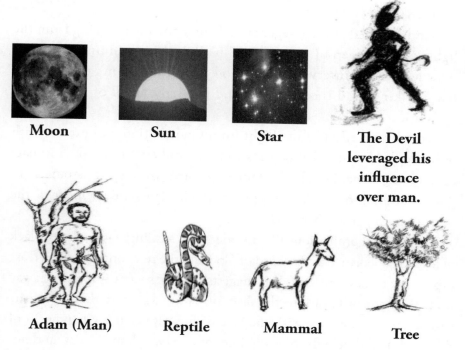

Moon

Sun

Star

The Devil leveraged his influence over man.

Adam (Man)

Reptile

Mammal

Tree

In obedience to Satan, man regarded creatures of God or his own handiwork as representations of God. Then he began to bow to them in worhsip. Unknowingly, man began the worship of Satan as though he was God.

Reaction of God to the foolishness of man

In response to the foolishness of man, God allowed him to do according to his desires for uncleanness; that in the lust of his heart he might remain darkness in the world of darkness.

So in ignorance, man believed that all was well with him.

Then he began to dishonour his body by defiling it with his behaviour towards others, and to worship and serve the creature rather than the Creator, who is blessed forever (Rom. 11:24–31). As if man had not bastardised his life enough, he then began to make covenant with death and with Sheol, and to make lies his refuge.

This gave rise to cultism in varied ways. The abominable practices became a trademark in the futility of self-importance and segregation of society into classes to oppress others (Ezek. 28:15, 18; Ezek. 8:10; 10:14, 16).

God watched as man degenerated and continued fleeing from the light into the deep of darkness. This flight is continuing until this day, despite the intervention of God at various points through the law, the kings and the prophets, and lastly the work of redemption by Jesus.

The adverse effect of the flight from God continues to expand with technology. Now married persons commit adultery not by the intimate act and lust alone, but also by initiating conversations with strangers to discuss nothing other than a rapport which suggests defilement of the heart of both parties (Mt. 5:28).

All other abominations like murder, lies, stealing, false witness, lack of love, disobedience of the word of God and the rest continue to increase exponentially day after day. This suggests that the society is speeding away from the light of God into the deep of darkness, where the end of the road is eternal romance with the lake of fire. (Reference Chapter 38 of this book.) God help us to be disciples of our Lord Jesus Christ, and not followers (John 20:22).

The Greatest of all Sins which is committed by Man.

This is the sin of abuse against his own body, which is sexual immorality (1 Cor. 6:18). The reason is that God has purchased the body with a prize – the blood of Jesus (1 Cor. 6:19, 20). Therefore, flee adultery and fornication by emotional action through taking stranger into your house and heart. This sin nowadays often hides behind seemingly harmless affectionate rapport via social media or technology connect leading to lust eventually (Heb. 3:6, 12). So keep body in santification and honour to God who avenges all who reject His Holy Spirit that he has given to Man (1 Thes. 4:3, 8).

The period when man walked alone

God watched man   **Sinful man**

Despite giving man space to do what pleased him, God has not at any time abandoned him totally, according to His promise (Heb. 13:5). This has spanned all the way through from when God drove man out of the Garden of Eden, to the era of Abel, Noah and Abraham, up to Jesus and eventually now.

The thoughts of God towards man have always been for a better future and hope (Jer. 29:11). Therefore He intermittently flashed this goodness towards man, that he might be awakened to recognise the blessings from Him. This has sustained the existence of man, even though he seemed to have failed to notice the mercy of God, and to believe in Him (2 Peter 1:19).

However, the hope for man took root when God found one man of faith who was known initially as Abram.

It is believed that Abram was the first to fully notice the entreaties of

God. The man Abram believed. So God accounted his belief to him for righteousness, and He subsequently gave the gift of faith to him (Gen. 15:6).

God later changed Abram's name to Abraham, and he became the first man to whom God did not impute iniquity because there was no deceit in his heart (Gen. 32:2).

This began the era in which God, who commanded light to shine out of darkness, began to shine in the dark heart of man, that he who will believe the light of the gospel might learn to wait patiently on the Lord as a tree by the riverside (Ps. 1:3).

This is the description of surrender to the Lord which is the faith of man, and his response to the gift of faith by God (2 Pet. 1:1).

The light from God is the gift of faith (Acts 3:16). It operates in the realm of the Spirit of God. So for man to notice the light and respond to it, he too has to be in the same spirit realm. This is the essence of the surrender of self to the light of God. It requires man to abandon self-effort and yield to be drawn into the Spirit realm. In practice, obey the voice of the word of God without doubt and questioning, as did the Patriarchs for our learning (Hebrew 13).

It is this kind of behaviour which made all who had the faith of Abraham to be brothers and sisters who did the will of God to which Jesus alluded (Mt. 12:50).

This is a way to walk in the Spirit. The Patriarchs demonstrated it without their foreknowledge that the spirit nature of man is the true persona (2 Cor. 5:16). In this way they were able to produce the fruit of the Spirit in Israel (Gal. 5:22–23).

It was a marvellous faith, considering that their spirits were then entangled by sin to form the perverse flesh, or the body of sin (Rom. 6:6).

But now the reason to have the faith of Abraham is made simpler for the man who might believe in Jesus and choose to be a slave to righteousness (1 Cor. 9:27). This is because the body of sin which was previously formed through the bond between the evil spirit and the spirit of man has been cut off by Christ, or circumcised without hands, and the Spirit created in holiness and righteousness which the man who believes now receives from God is unencumbered.

Chapter Nine

The (unmerited) favour to Abram

Nothing suggests that Abram was not an Idol-worshipper.

Examination

There is no clear biblical record which differentiates Abram from his kinsmen who worshipped things created by God (Joshua 24:2).

Although God looks at the heart and not the physical body, the scripture suggests that Abram was an idol-worshipper until He called him. What God saw in him might be the explanation of why He called him alone to leave his father's house (Gen. 12:1). Abram obeyed but took his nephew, Lot, along on his way to the Promised Land (Gen 12:4).

However, God accounted the obedience of Abram to him for righteousness (Gen. 15:16; Rom. 4:3). Afterwards, God changed his name to Abraham (Gen. 17:5).

The unwavering belief of Abraham was akin to surrender to God. It earned him the alias of 'the father of faith' (Rom. 4:19–20).

This affirms that faith, in practical terms, is to surrender to the Lord.

It amounts to letting go of self-effort and allowing God to be responsible for leading, providing and doing all the other things of life for you while you stay at rest (1 Pet. 5:5–7).

The main promise of God to Abraham, beside earthly things, was the *blessing of the promise.* This was to bless all the families of the earth through him (Gen. 12:1–3).

It is worthy to observe that Abraham did not receive this principal promise in his lifetime on earth, but he received the promise of earthly things (Heb. 11:39).

This suggests that the 'blessing of the promise is what the gospel of grace is really about, and not the promise of earthly things.

The promise of a son to Abraham

Abraham

**Isaac
(the promised son)**

Abraham was a hundred years old and his wife Sarah was ninety when Isaac was born. This laid the foundation for the fulfilment of the promise of God that through Abraham the world shall be blessed (Gen. 12:3).

This blessing was to be through the righteousness of faith, and not through the righteousness of the law (Phil. 3:9; Rom. 4:13). It was to be of faith so that salvation might be according to grace, to all the seeds of

Abraham throughout the entire world (Rom. 4:16). This suggests that righteousness was equally imputed for all who shall believe in God, who raised our Lord Jesus Christ from the dead (Rom. 4:24).

God examined the faith of Abraham

In what seemed to be a test of faith, God commanded Abraham to sacrifice his only son, Isaac, to Him (Gen. 22:2).

This was definitely not temptation because Abraham had nothing to benefit from it. Rather, it was to test Abraham's obedience in a critical situation of self-denial. The difference is that temptation breeds gain (Mt. 4:3) but test puts man in a situation that might require him to show whether he is disposed to self denial and unconditional love or lack of them in the face of deprivation or something capable of attracting agony and sorrow to him.

Father and son on the journey to make the sacrifice

Firewood

Along the way Isaac enquired about the sacrificial lamb, but Abraham replied that God would provide (Gen. 22:7).

Isaac   **Abraham**

Abraham about to sacrifice Isaac at Mount Moriah

Abraham

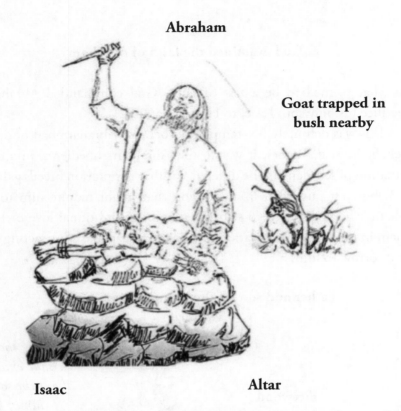

Goat trapped in bush nearby

Isaac　　　　　　　　　**Altar**

Abraham prepared to sacrifice his son, Isaac. In the nick of time, God stopped Abraham (Gen, 22:10–12). Instead God provided a goat entangled in the bush nearby for the sacrifice (Gen. 22:13).

This action testified to Abraham's faith in God (James 2:22). It proved to God that there is hope for his foreordained salvation of man (Rom. 8:29).

The surrender of Abraham to God brought to the fore the glory of God as supreme (Heb. 11:17–19). This was by believing that God could raise Isaac from the dead, from where he received him earlier to according to the promise.

Special Place in Mount Moriah

One thousand years after Abraham's sacrifice (Gen, 22:2) King David faltered by conducting censor in disobedience to the word of God. The error attracted plague of death upon the people. As a remedy God made David to buy the the threshing floor of Ornan the Jebusite. There he built altar to offer sacrifice, prayers and worship to the Lord. God heard him and put an end to the plague (2 Sam, 24: 24-25). So the site became 'house of prayer' and temple of sacrifice (Is. 56:7). It turned out to be Mount Moriah (2 Chr. 3:11). It was on it that Solomon built the temple in Jerusalem (1 Chr. 21:28). It was at the site Jesus was crucified and it is from there He will rule on Earth in the future (Is. 2:2-4).

Unmerited favour to the Jews continued

The Law was engraved with the finger of God on Tablet at Mount Sinnai (Ex. 20:1-17)

Moses leading Isreal out of Egypt and into the promise land

The Journey witnessed signs and wonders due to the glory of God in form of cloud or fire upon them. Their approach made sea to flee, Jordan to roll back, mountains and hills to skip and quake, and water to flow out of the rock et al (Ps. 114).

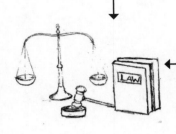

Moses made two trips and stayed forty days and nights each time in Mount Sinnai (Ex. 20:1-17)

The giving of the law

Some four hundred and twenty years after Abraham, God chose Moses to led Israel out of Egypt after about four hundred and thirty years of their bondage (Ex. 12:40). The destination was the promise land of Canaan, the land of their pilgrimage, and as stranger, which God in the past assured the Patriarchs (Ex. 6:4).

On their way to the promise land, Moses appointed judges over the people. All agreed to obey the voice of God and to keep His covenant (Ex. 19:8).

Afterwards God called Moses to Mount Sinai and gave him two tablets of Ten Commandments.

While he was up on the mountain forty days and nights on his first trip, the people made golden calf with their jewelry and began to worship it as their god.

On return Moses broke the tablets in anger. It is believed this was to prevent God's destruction of all the people for disobeying the law.

Then God commanded Moses to sift the people and three thousand men died by the sword of Levite the same day (Ex. 32:28).

It made the law to be regarded as the ministry of death (2Cor. 3:6).

On his 2nd trip Moses brought the Ten Commandments to Israel (Ex. 20:1-17). The people chorused to do what God said (Ex. 24:3).

This subjected them as wife to the righteousness of the law as their tutor and husband.

But they were unable to obey the law (Acts 15:10).

However the law was good but not perfect. So God had to afterwards execute the perfect scheme, which is Jesus crucified (1Cor. 2:2).

The purpose of the law

The law was given to bring man to the knowledge of sin. It was therefore intended to make man see the evil of self-righteousness and the need to turn to the righteousness of the law for refuge for a time. This switch is the marriage of man as wife by the spirit within him to the law of Moses as his husband.

Therefore the prime purpose of the law was to teach man the way of the Lord; then prepare him for the imminent worship by faith which was to come through the seed of Abraham (Gal. 3:24).

Aftermath of the law

Israel switched from living according to self-righteousness to living by the righteousness of the law (Rom. 7:1).

So Israel turned to the worship of God by the ark of tabernacle with the sacrifice of animal blood accompanied with ceremonies and rituals. The eleven tribes who received land for inheritance were under command to pay obligatory tithe to the Levite tribe, which God chose to serve as priest at the altar for their inheritance (Num. 18:21). The inheritance was not transferable (Num. 36:6).

This suggests that ministers under the gospel of grace have no justification to demand for tithe because their inheritance is not earthly things but Christ. Tithe as an inheritance was specific to the Levites and Abraham was not chosen by God as priest when he paid tithe to Melchizedek.

Under the law the Pharisees and teachers of the law formulated own traditional regulations which in the process undermined the Ten Commandments. Examples are washing of hands before eating (Mt. 15:2), and fasting by abstinence from food and drink, etc. (Mt. 9:14).

On the other hand, the Gentiles continued to live according to self-righteousness and the wisdom of the world, without God and law in their existence.

Chapter Ten

Prophecy of the Coming of God to Earth

God has not abandoned man to himself at any time from when He drove him out of the Garden of Eden. The moment Adam disobeyed God He immediately laid out His preordained plan to redeem him from sin. In pursuit of this promise He declared that the Seed of a woman will bruise the head of the serpent, the Devil who is also known as Satan (Gen. 3:15). Afterwards God gave the law to Israel, which carved a special relationship with Him. Throughout the period of the law the Gentiles lived in self-righteousness while Israel lived in the righteousness of the law. All along, the mystery Seed was at work behind the scenes. He was responsible for the miraculous parting of the Red Sea, the healing by the bronze serpent, and so on (Num. 21:9).

In order to let man be aware of the unfolding mystery Seed of God, He spoke to Israel through prophecies from the mouths of the prophets, the priests and the kings. But the hardness of the heart of man did not allow him to see the essence of the prophecy, even though he had desired to know the mystery (Lk. 10:24).

Eventually God was manifested on earth in the form of ordinary man (1 Tim. 3:16). Many years earlier it was prophesied that He would be born a commoner (Phil. 2:7–8). All prophecies were fulfilled to the letter by Jesus. This suggests that He was the indisputable true God of heaven who came to earth.

Amongst the prophecies were:
* The birth
* The ministry
* The suffering
* The persecution of the innocent for the sins which man committed
* The death by way of hanging
* The revival of man after two days in death (Hosea 6:2)
* The resurrection
* The ascension to heaven of Christ Jesus

Even the manner of His ascension to heaven was prophesied to be different from the way He came to earth (1 Kings 13:17): Prophet Isaiah wrote that He would come by way of conception and birth by a virgin (Mary) (Is. 7:14), and that He would ascend into heaven in bodily form (Lk. 24:51).

Our healing from transgressions was ordained by God according to the prophecy of Prophet Isaiah (Is. 53:5). This was fulfilled with the thirty-nine stripes, with a maximum of forty permitted, less one as per Jewish law (Deut. 25:1–3).

The healing by the stripes which cut chunks of flesh out of the body of Jesus was echoed by Apostle Peter (1 Pet. 2:24). Apostle Paul equally bore the maximum number of stripes, five times (2 Cor. 11:24).

Jesus is 100% God and 100% man

In the belly of Prophet Isaiah's prophecy that *unto us a child is born, and unto us a Son is given (Is. 9:6a, 9:6b)* lies the most amazing wisdom.

Simply put, the child that was born was the god of the image and likeness of God in the order of the first Adam at creation (1 Cor. 15:47a). The Son that was given was the Son of Man of the Lord who came down from heaven above (Ps. 2:7; 1 Cor. 15:47b).

This cohesion of the Son of Man of the Lord, and God of the image and likeness of God, forms the dual personality of Jesus as fully (100%) God and fully (100%) man (John 3:31; John 8:23).

It is the Son of Man that is the bread of God who comes down from heaven and who gives life to the world (John 6:33). He is equally the God who has been given all authority in heaven and on earth (Mt. 28:18). This stockade is symbolised by the common thread of Divinity in these three statements, thus:

1. The Spirit of God descended from heaven like a dove and remained upon Jesus immediately after His baptism (Mt. 3:16–17).
2. Jesus had the power to lay down His life and to take it again (John 10:7–18), which He did respectively before He breathed His last on the cross (Lk. 23:46), and after resurrection (Ps. 31:5)
3. He bodily ascended after the resurrection (Acts 1:9–10)

The dual nature was prophesied by Zechariah (Zech. 13:7c), and it was fulfilled by Jesus (John 14:9). Prophet Micah was precise on the birthplace of Bethlehem (Mic. 5:2), and it came to pass (Mt. 2:1–2). Prophet Isaiah was equally precise on the name of the Son of God as Immanuel (Is 7:14), and it came to be (Mt. 1:18–23).

God hinted in His promise to Abram that in him all the families of the earth shall be blessed (Gen. 12:3c), and today Jesus has indeed become the blessing to all nations (Acts 3:25–26), even though anybody has the choice to count himself out.

The prophecy that the Messiah will be in the order of the Melchizedek priesthood (Gen. 14:18) has been equally fulfilled by Christ as the high priest (Heb. 6:20).

The saying by Abraham that God will provide the lamb of sacrifice (Gen. 22:8) was fulfilled when God gave His only begotten Son to the world as a Lamb of sacrifice (John 1:29). Even the last supper which Melchizedek mimicked with Abraham (Gen. 14:18) was fulfilled when Jesus performed the last supper with His disciples (Mt. 26:26–29). The prophecy which linked Judah to Jesus (Gen. 49:10) came to be with the birth of Jesus by Mary, who was of the lineage of Judah (Lk. 3:33).

The prophecy that not a bone of the Lamb will be broken (Ex. 12:46) came to pass (John 19:31–36). So also was the prophecy that the healing power of the Messiah will be in the wings (Mal. 4:2) proved by the miraculous healing of the woman with the issue of blood (Mt. 9:20–22).

Even Prophet Isaiah prophesied His lowly upbringing as a mere man who would be rejected, and persecuted with untold suffering; but will be filled with healing power; and lastly be the sins which man had committed, and sacrificed and killed by crucifixion to provide the peace of God to man, buried but resurrected, and so on (Is. 53:1–12). All these prophecies were fulfilled to the letter by Jesus (Phil. 2:7–8; 2 Cor. 5:21).

As Moses raised a bronze serpent as a healing remedy for all who suffered from a snake bite to look at (Num. 21:9), even so Jesus was lifted up to draw all men to Himself that they might be saved (John 3:14–16). The prophecy that *cursed is the man who hangs on the tree* (Deut. 21:23) was fulfilled by the crucifixion of Jesus on a tree (Gal. 3:13). Some other prophecies which were fulfilled included the crucifixion as prophesied by

Prophet Isaiah (Is. 2:7–8) and fulfilled by Jesus in Acts 13:29–30.

Then the life through faith in Jesus was prophesied by King David (Ps. 2:12) and fulfilled in John 20:31.

That Jesus would be forsaken because of the sins of others was prophesied by King David (Ps. 22:1) and it was fulfilled when God turned His back on Him on the cross, that man might become the righteousness of God in Him (2 Cor. 5:21).

The listing of the prophecies and their corresponding fulfilment by Jesus may run into hundreds in number when fully determined.

What this suggests is that the grace which came through Jesus has its root in the mystery of the Old Testament. Thus the pathway which the mystery Seed described throughout the Old Testament defines the most relevant aspect of the Old to the gospel of grace.

This is more apt for the purpose of validating the credibility of the gospel of Jesus crucified (Gal. 1:1, 11).

Chapter Eleven

Fasting in the Eye of God

Why fast?

The purpose of fasting is to make the heart pure in preparation to meet God or to do His will. Its origin can be traced to the preparation to receive God on the day of convocation for atonement (Lev. 16:29–30).

It was then understood to be abstinence from pleasure (food, drink and sex). It suggests that man at that time lacked the knowledge of the demand of fasting. However, God put up with man's understanding that the soul is afflicted by abstinence from indulgences. Certainly it is the body and not the soul that is afflicted. Under the law abstinence, putting on of sack cloth and ashes was regarded as repentance (Jonah 3:5-10).

Nonetheless, God frowned at the way man fasted by abstinence (Is. 58:5). It is only God's chosen fast that will afflict the soul and cleanse the heart, and make it pure.

The observable proof of a pure heart is the outflowing of love to fellow neighbours, which is the only thing a man is forever to owe anybody (Rom. 13:8).

The reason is that it is the show of love that will raise the hope of the beneficiary to have a sense of belonging, and so give thanks to God.

On the other hand, the benefactor's heart is filled with joy and pleasing to God. This is because the love which is shown to the brother who is around is like the love shown to God, whom we do not see (1 John 4:20).

Love reduces hate, rancour, etc. in society. In this way the heart is made pure and pleasing to God, who looks only at the heart (1 Sam. 16:7)

Moreover, love makes both the benefactor and the beneficiary look to God as the sole great provider, who deserves praise and thanksgiving at all times (Phi. 4:19; Ps. 23:1). This is pleasing to God.

Fasting under the law: abstinence from meals

Man fasting, turns back on food

Fasting is to this day seen through the prism of the law of Moses (Est. 4:16).

But God has disproved this fasting, which many have accepted as real (Is. 58:5). Indeed, the scripture say that fasting by abstinence is in error (Zech. 7:5–6).

To stick to the mode of fasting under the law suggests an outright hardness of the heart of man. It is like a deliberate defiance of God, who has spoken against abstinence through the prophets (Zech. 1:4; 7:7). Jesus was unmistakable in pointing to what is fasting and the sacredness of it under grace. He alluded to fasting as a means of purifying the heart when He said that His word made the hearts of His disciples pure as long as He was with them (John 15:3). Additionally, Jesus made it known that the old way of fasting is not compatible with the fast chosen by God from times past (Lk. 5:34–39).

Whether a man eats and drinks or not is for himself and not for God (Zech. 7:6). What God instructed man to do to fast even under the law was to obey His words to bring burnt offerings and sacrifices, grain offerings and incense and sacrifices of praise to the house of the Lord (Jer. 17:26).

At best fasting by abstinence might be considered a test of endurance of hunger. This has the devastating effect of lowering man's energy and effectiveness at work, which impairs sound reasoning and vision.

Abstinence from food and drink is believed to be an act of self-righteousness. Food will not purify the heart because whatever is ingested is later passed out of the body without it touching the heart (Mt. 15:11).

The fasting chosen by God:

Illustration of the chosen fast
References: Is. 58:6–7; Mt. 25:35–36, 40; Lk. 4:18–19.

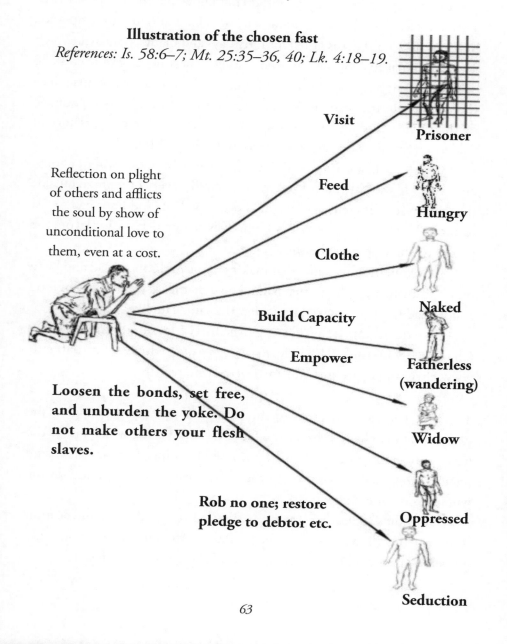

Reflection on plight of others and afflicts the soul by show of unconditional love to them, even at a cost.

Visit — Prisoner

Feed — Hungry

Clothe — Naked

Build Capacity

Empower — Fatherless (wandering)

Loosen the bonds, set free, and unburden the yoke. Do not make others your flesh slaves.

Widow

Rob no one; restore pledge to debtor etc.

Oppressed

Seduction

The scripture says: *My people are destroyed for lack of knowledge* (Hos. 4:6). Fasting by abstinence is a good example of this pronouncement.

The fast chosen by God is simple and is affordable by all classes of people – both the rich and the poor in material possessions and in learning.

This is simply to *show love to all men in the likeness of Jesus* (1 John 2:6).

It is regrettable that many people do not know that Jesus did not fast by abstinence from food, but by the chosen fast of God prior to His temptation by Satan (Lk. 5:33). Jesus fasted for forty days and nights in the wilderness. The traditional fixation of mind on fasting as abstinence from food and drink often suggests the old way of fasting under the law. Of course there was no food in the wilderness. The sorry frame of mind is compounded by the Devil tempting Jesus to turn stone to bread. The circumstance of wilderness further hides the real essence of fasting behind the veil.

In brief, Jesus was born and lived as a man with a free will of choice. So before He was baptised of water, He lived like every other man outside the will of God. Therefore, to begin to do the will of God Jesus had to fast to make His heart pure towards God. This required Him to devote the period to chewing over the chosen fast.

This temptation was aimed at making Jesus to disobey God and be in return disowned by The Father. Satan knew that Jesus was hungry of food and he had hoped to make Him suffer the same fate like Adam.

(The detail of Jesus' fasting for forty days and nights is in Chapter 38 of the 2013 title *Return to God*, which is available at www.christthelordreign.com for free online reading)

To show love to others is to demonstrate an unfettered giving to the needy what man has received from God. It is this fasting which makes the heart pure, and so fulfils the real purpose of fasting. In practice: ensure justice, show mercy according to the righteousness of Christ and do the will of God (Mic. 6:8).

Under the law fasting was primarily tied to the day of convocation to prepare for the visit of God on the day of Atonement. But under the gospel of grace God lives in man, and so fasting is to be a lifestyle.

This is why it is recommended to anoint the head with washed face while fasting. It is to make fasting an affairs of the heart in the service to God and not to attract attention of people to self (Mt. 6:17–18). This hides the intention from onlookers, as well as denying oneself the praise of men while letting God alone know the purpose of fasting as a service to Him (Ruth 3:3).

Chapter Twelve

The Mystery Seed of Abraham

The son which God promised to give to Abraham was born as Isaac, and in him was the mystery Seed of Abraham. This Seed of promise was next borne in the loins of Jacob, the son of Isaac, and then in sequence by Ruth and Boaz of the tribe of Judah, followed by Obey, and finally by King David. Then the trend of journey changed from the line of heir apparent to the throne of David to Nathan, one of the sons of King David. In Nathan's lineage was Mary, the wife of Joseph, who himself was a descendant of Solomon, the son of David. Mary, being a woman, could not make herself pregnant. This suggests that the bearer of the Seed of Abraham passed over from humanity in King David to spirituality in God. Finally the Holy Spirit planted the Seed of promise in Mary, the daughter of Joachim of the lineage of King David (Lk.1:35), and wife of Joseph. Lastly, the virgin Mary gave birth to the Seed of promise, who is Jesus, the saviour of mankind (Lk. 2:11) and now our master (Mt. 23:10).

| Joseph | Jesus | Mary |
| (Father) | (Baby) | (Mother) |

The baptism of Jesus

At age thirty, John the Baptist baptised Jesus by immersion in the water of the River Jordan. (Mt. 3:13-16).

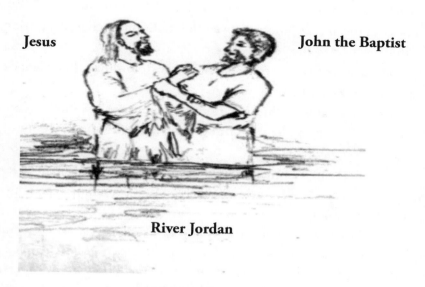

Jesus   **John the Baptist**

River Jordan

Observations

Water baptism is a symbol to identify with the kingdom of God.

John the Baptist used it to point out Jesus to the Jews as the Lamb of God who takes away the sin of the world (John 1:29).

The first time Jesus was attested to as the Son of God by a voice from heaven was immediately after the baptism of John the Baptist (Mt. 3:17).

Jesus was born in the similar manner in which God created Adam and this made Him to be regarded as the second Adam

*However unlike Jesus who is the **Word of God** by virtue of His nature, Adam was god by virtue of his creation as a **desire of God**.*

Another difference is that Jesus has the Spirit of God. But Adam had own spirit which God formed within him and gave him self-will (Zech.12:1b; as another speaking personality in the image and likeness of God (Gen. 1:26-27).

Key points to note in the first coming of Jesus.

God *predetermined the work to save man and Jesus volunteered to do it (Lk. 1:70-75; 22:22).* It put an end to the purpose of the ark of the Lord on earth (Jer. 3:16).

The work to save man was proposed to give life back to him (Lk. 4:18).

Jesus was born under the law of Moses and as a result the prevailing practices and traditions were followed in His upbringing (Lk. 2:39). This does not mean that Jesus approved the tradition, such as dedication, and tithing as part of the gospel of grace.

At the age of twelve years He showed extraordinary knowledge of the scripture (Lk. 2:49).

Jesus was baptised through immersion in water by John the Baptist in the River Jordan to identify Him to man and with the kingdom of God (Mt. 3:16–17).

Jesus was tempted by the Devil in a similar manner to Adam (Mt. 4:3–10).

Afterwards He went around teaching and preaching repentance and the kingdom of God (Mt. 4:17).

Jesus preached His core messages in parables to conceal the truth from the generality of man. This was to allow only those men whom God found and called to the fold to understand and receive the benefits of the teaching (Mark 4:11). It is in a similar way that the truth of the New Testament gospel is concealed. This is to ensure that it is only by the Holy Spirit it is understood that the glory might be of God and not man (2 Cor. 4:3–4).

Jesus accompanied the mission with visible healing and miracles to show the power and mercy of God to the sinners (1 Cor. 1:22). As important as physical healing is, it was not the reason for His coming (Mk. 1:38).

In like manner, His remark with respect to the law of Moses was not an approval or condemnation of it, but was made to obey the law of the day (Lk. 18:12).

Jesus deliberately set a path to the kingdom of God for man to learn and follow (Mt. 5:3–16). Jesus was without sin, but later became the sins previously committed by man (2 Cor. 5:21).

For this reason He was crucified and buried. But God raised Him from the dead three days later (Rom. 6:4–5) to become our saviour and head of His church.

Chapter Thirteen

The Riddle of Giving and Seed-sowing

Giving

To give is different to sowing seed. To sow seed is to aim at a change in the orientation of man, and to seek continued increase in all ways towards God.

But to give is to aim at thanksgiving, praise and glory to God for what He has done. It helps to further the works of sowing seed. In both cases God assuredly does the refilling (Prov. 19:17). Giving has the capacity to win soul of the receiver. He may use what he has received to partake in seed-sowing to others. Giving might lead the beneficiary to give thanks to God for His goodness to him through the benefactor, whom God will continue to increase (Prov. 11:24).

Seed-sowing

The scripture clearly defines a seed as the word of God (Lk. 8: 11). This suggests that there is a difference between seed in the view of God and in the view of man. When this is not recognised, there might be the tendency to regard giving and seed-sowing as the same. The result will be a mixture of the things of God with the things of man.

Render therefore to Caesar the things that are Caesar's and to God the things that are GOD's (Lk. 20:25).

Mixture of any kind suggests a disaster in how a disciple of Jesus, and not a Christian, reads the scripture and how he conducts himself. *Certainly there is a difference between a disciple and a Christian.*

The parable of the sower was based on the service of faith which a certain woman showed for the love of God (Lk. 7:44–47).

Illustration

Group A1. As he sowed, some seed fell by wayside and were trampled down, and birds ate it (Luke 8:5).

**Religious man
(law)**

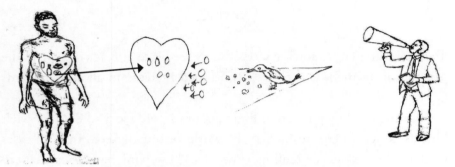

A mind set on law and own scheme. Unbelieving soul lacks knowledge of truth. Regards word as threat to old belief Resists change for fear of losing exalted place he now enjoys. Doubt the word and woks against it.	**Fowls of the air (the Devil) devour the word by sowing doubt and contradicting the word heard making hearing unwilling to accept (Lk. 8:12)**	**Sower of the seed, or word of God (Rom. 10:13–18). This word is of planting things of Kingdom of God and righteousness in heart of man by vocal and behaviour,**

Group A1.1. Later:

**Religious man
(law)**

Heart rejects the word. Focus on self, not willing to let others know. So word will not profit him and there will not be fruit to Harvest by Jesus.

Group A2. The seed that fell on rock, which soon withered (Lk. 8:6)

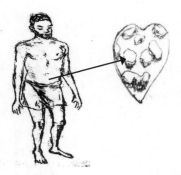

**Religious man
(tradition)**

- Hears the word with joy, but expects quick change in his condition and finds it is not happening so.
- **He will not persevere.**
- So skepticism sets in. And loses the initial hope, joy and peace.
- Swayed by temptation, persecution and then will deny the word of truth.
- Rather lusts for earthly things: riches, fame & power.
- Return to wat of greed, manipulative etc.

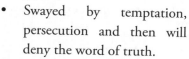

**Preachers
Voice**

Group A2.1. Later

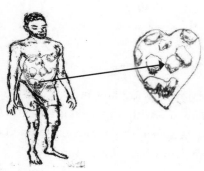

**Religious man
(tradition)**

- Heart has no place for the word of God.
- It is busy with issues of own religion, the issues of this world and lust for them with passion (John 2:15-16).
- It is pre-occupied with self-preservation which overrides the word. Therefore it will deny Jesus.
- Since the word did not take root there will be neither fruit nor crop to harvest after all.

Group A3. The seed sowed which fell

**Lukewarm
man**

- Hears the word of God and he
- receives it with gladness.
- But he has no time to give it full
- attention as required by God..
- To make up, he designs own
- gospel out of the word: This
- may lead to gospel of
- motivation, matrimony, and
- prosperity which fit into the
- desires of people of the world.
- Double minded heart, that
- regards the word as means of
- gain (1Tim 6:9-10).
- Half baked heart which thinks
- he is well informed of the truth.
- But delights in pleasure and in
- self-preservation (Lk. 8:14).
- Soon forgets the word and
- gets entangled by own desires.

Preacher's Voice

Group A3.1. Later

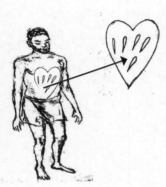

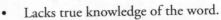

- Lacks true knowledge of the word.
- Presumptuous and with own agenda (Mt. 7:22-23.)
- Believes the 'preacher' or statements creditted to past Clergy more than what the scripture says.
- Enjoys activities unrelated to the word in local gathering which is meant for the worship of God.
- Ruminate more on benefits of earthly things. etc.
- Believes he is doing much in the name of Jesus but unaware it is contrary to the word of God.

Preacher's voice

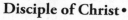

- Hears the word of God and believes absolutely.
- Keeps and lives by them (Lk. 8:15; Joshua 1:8)

Disciple of Christ •

- Good ground. The heart dwells more on word of God. Strive to be Christ-like and be righteousness of God in Him.
- Has **understanding** of the word of God
- Promotes the spread of the gospel of Jesus crucified alone (1Cor. 2:2) by supporting outreach programmes to win lost souls to Christ (3Johb 8).

Group A4.1. Later

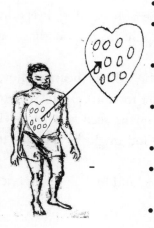

- Heart full of peace of God
- Fellowships with Christ by faith. This is to surrender to Him. To submit to God
- builds faith by which man can stand in the grace of God, (Rom. 5:2).
- Body, spirit and soul will be in harmony, etc (1Thes. 5:23)
- The man grows in knowledge of God.
- He lives a pious life, seeks to make disciples of men by any means open to him.
- Produces fruit of the spirit (Gal. 5:22-23).
- Ready for the second coming of Christ any day.

The parable of seed-sowing by the preacher, and the service rendered by the woman who washed the feet of Jesus with her tears and wiped them with the hair of her head and so on (Lk. 7: 44–46), describe the two ways to sow seed:

1. The case of the woman is known as *seed-sowing by instinctive service to God*. Another example is the case of the Good Samaritan (Lk. 10: 33–35). Every gift without expecting benefit from any quarter, not even from God, falls into this class (Gal. 6–10).
2. The case of the preacher is known as *seed-sowing by spreading the word of the kingdom to please God*. Another example is the Apostle Peter's choice to dedicate himself to the spreading of the word, and not to serve table (Acts 6:4).

The objective of seed-sowing is to make the kingdom of God known to people.

This suggests that any giving where return is expected, from either man or God, is not seed-sowing to the kingdom but an 'investment'.

Jesus further insinuated that seed-sowing is a heart experience. It is a matter of letting God be the judge and the beneficiary of the glory and thanksgiving.

As shown in the illustrations, four different groups of heart, possibilities and significance exist in the exercise of seed-sowing (Lk. 8:11–15).

So for the seed to survive, the heart has to be void of any toxin that might hamper growth, and be willing. That is, a heart without deceit regarding the source of the seed and the purpose of its sowing. It is only the seed having life which is received legitimately from God that can satisfy the criteria (Joshua 1:8; Is. 55:10).

On the other hand, the hearer has to also be willing (heart without wicked intent, but of thanksgiving and surrender to God) for the seed to take root and grow. Therefore the purpose of sowing seed is not to seek gain or fame or recognition by man, but that God might be revealed to men (1 Tim. 6:5; Gal. 1:10).

Seed is to be sowed in both love and in tears, and by habitual service (Ps. 136:5–6).

Chapter Fourteen

The Real Bread of Life

The life in this instance is not the life that man lives on earth. Rather, the life is the life which is lived in the kingdom of God. There in the kingdom Jesus is the bread and drink of the true life of man. This man is he whom God has adjudged worthy to be a citizen of His kingdom, which on earth is hidden within the earthly man.

Jesus as the bread of life is represented in concrete terms by the word of God. It is this word of God that became flesh (John 1:14). This makes the flesh the true bread of life from heaven (John 6:50). Now the word spoken by Jesus is life (John 6:63).

This suggests that the flesh of Christ is His written word, which makes up the scripture. So to eat the flesh is to take in and ruminate on the word of God. This is the real bread that is required to feed the soul. So, all that is required to eat the bread is to study the Holy Bible (Joshua 1:8).

It is this alone that will quench the hunger and thirst of the soul to make a sacrifice of the mortal form. Thus eating the prophetic word leads man to come to the knowledge of God who shone in his dark heart to shine the light of knowledge of His glory in the face of Jesus (2 Cor. 4:6). So every instance which requires man to eat the flesh and drink the blood of Jesus Christ centres on the study and rumination on the written word of God (John 6:53–54).

Jesus

What it takes to eat and drink the blood of Jesus

Thirsty – quench by meditation

Hungry – satisfy by study

Meditating on the word of God which has been studied portrays assent to Christ's spoken word. By agreeing with the message you are sipping in what it is set to achieve. In this way you are drinking the blood, in which consists the life of the flesh of Christ (Lev. 17:11). Meditation calls for quietness and wait in hope to hear the truth from the Holy Spirit while ponder the word (Lk. 11:28). The Holy Spirit is the water that Jesus gives (John 7:38–39). The water builds in man the wisdom and knowledge of God, which He has put in Christ for him (Mt. 7:11, 21:22).

Study takes three stages:
1. First *seek* to find the apt scriptures.
2. *Knock* by the reading of the word.
3. *Ask* for the truth by digesting the read to get the truth.

The three constitute the flesh of the incarnated Jesus. Then assimilate the truth as food, which is the flesh of Jesus that builds the soul. It is the bread that will satisfy the soul more than mortal food will for the body (Lk. 12:23). To study and assimilate the truth is a show of faith or submission to God and Christ Jesus (John 6:35).

Chapter Fifteen

The Exchange of Rights Between Jesus and Man

Why Jesus washed the disciples' feet

It is not a secret that many Christians believe that Jesus washed the feet of His disciples to teach man how to be humble and to be a servant to others.

This is true to a lesser degree because it suggests the viewpoint of human wisdom (Lk. 22:27) conjoured with suggestion by the word of God. *The more fundamental reason for the ritual lies in the Jewish tradition.*

Let us see why it was desirable for Jesus to wash the feet of man (John 13:5–12). The law established as the brother of man the principle of redemption of the poor who has been bonded to a rich sojourner or stranger. It declared that he may be redeemed by his brother or whoever is near of Kin to him that is capable (Lev. 25: 47-51).

The purpose was to set the regime for Jesus to do the will of God by taking away the law and establishing His blood covenant for the gospel of grace (Heb. 10:9).

First is that the Jewish tradition gives the right of first choice to the man who is recognised to have the right of possession to redeem what is at stake. Where he is unwilling or incapable, he can give up his rights to someone who is willing and able to take up the challenge to redeem the rights for self. This agreement is sealed by the incapable man pulling off his shoe for the rescuer to wash his feet (Ruth 4:8–10).

In the case of the man and Jesus, the man had the right of first choice to save himself. But he was unable (Ps. 49:6–8), because to save himself required him to forgive himself as the offender, recant his disobedience to God, heal his own broken heart, and free himself from captivity and oppression by the Devil, which requires the sacrifice of his soul to God. Then educate himself about his own origin and know the truth, restore his own blinded spiritual sight, unburden his darkness and so on (Lk. 4:18). Unable to do these things, man gave up his rights to Jesus, who was willing to accept to redeem man for Himself. This is the parable which the acceptance by the disciples for Jesus to wash their feet spiritually represents.

Therefore, washing the feet of the disciples by Jesus symbolised His acceptance to be the guilt of man, or the sins previously committed (2 Cor. 5:21). It justified Jesus to shed His blood and to be the propitiation by His blood through faith. *By it, God showed His righteousness through His forgiveness of the sins that were previously committed (Rom. 3:25).* This suggests why Jesus, on the cross, pleaded with God to forgive His adversaries because they did not know what they were doing (Lk. 23:34).

Additionally, God later affirmed the forgiveness by giving His righteousness and the spirit of Christ to man, that he might live his life for Him (Gal. 2:20).

The last supper of Jesus with the disciples

Last Supper

The import of the last supper can be described as the response of Jesus to the 'honour' done to Him by man for accepting Him to wash his feet

Thus the last supper served to reciprocate the gesture of man by giving to him His right of the righteousness of God, using bread and wine as symbols. *It represented the enactment of the new covenant with the precious blood of the Lamb (Heb. 10:16).*

The ritual signalled the removal of the wall of separation erected by sin and ordinances. Additionally, it sealed the reconciliation of man to God through Jesus Christ (2 Cor. 5:18–19).

Henceforth, till the end of His passion Jesus became poor, that through His poverty man might become rich in righteousness (Rom. 9:23).

It is very significant to understand this poverty of Jesus to overcome the mistake of believing that the scripture means the poverty of mortal possessions (2 Cor. 8:9).

The reciprocal exchange fostered a bond between man and Jesus Christ as friends and as one body (1 Cor. 10:17).

The demand of "Do this in remembrance of Me" (Jesus)

The Jews have kept fate with the command of God to them to observe every year the Passover feast in Egypt (Ex. 12:22).

It was on the occasion of celebrating that Passover feast that Jesus had the last supper with His disciples. Then he similarly commended that man should do same as often as possible in remembrance of Him (Lk. 22:19).

The centre of attention in this command is the remembrance of the salvation from death to life of the man God created in the beginning (2 Cor. 5:21).

This man is the invisible masterpiece of treasure which God made in His own DNA. He is currently hidden within the human form (2 Cor. 5:1) and has been a prisoner of sin and a slave to sin since the time in Eden when Adam first committed sin.

Now Jesus has set him free to receive the award and the investiture of the righteousness of God in Christ (Rom. 3:22).

So this remembrance is particularly to celebrate this freedom as well as the Lord Jesus Christ who made it possible. It is a personalised thing, but it will be merrier with a group of like mind in Christ Jesus (Acts 2:42, 46).

This suggests that it is not a ritual of painstaking practice with a peculiar meal of any description. *It is a celebration which demands a mind focused on the passion of Jesus for our freedom from the Devil and reconciliation with God through Christ (2 Cor. 5:19).*

After Christ Jesus was raised, He demonstrated the celebration of remembrance of Him at Emmaus with two disciples (Lk. 24:30). Then He repeated it at the seashore with more of His disciples for our learning (John 21:15–17).

These examples suggest that the most significant expectation in the remembrance of Jesus is the reflection on the philosophy of Jesus crucified. It involves dwelling on the words of God concerning the crucifix. The word is the true bread or body of Jesus, common to all that have believed (John 6:58; 1 Cor. 10:17). A true Christian regards self according to the spirit in the same way that Christ is now regarded according to the Spirit (2Cor. 5:16). This suggests that the true bread and wine which is fit for the remembrance of Jesus is the bread from heaven. Thus using material bread and wine might suggest the mixing of the affairs of spirit personalities with the table of demons (1 Cor. 10:21).

Additionally, ponder on the marred body of Jesus on the cross, that the man who might believe in Him will be saved (Ps. 22:14–18; Is. 52:14).

This may further be examined differently, but with the same result: as someone who has been raised with Christ, the believer is a spirit just like Christ is now. It is therefore required of him who has been raised from the dead to walk and talk like one in the spirit (2 Cor. 5:16). This suggests that it is needless to look back to the earthly ritual of man in the flesh, which contrasts the faith of man in God (Lk. 9:62).

What Jesus did with material bread and wine was a one-off ceremony. Thus it was concluded once forever to mark the covenant He made with His blood. In that occasion both Jesus and man were in the form of earthly being.

That one-off ritual cleared the way once and forever, for all that might receive the righteousness of God in Christ. It is an area in which man until now has required better understanding.

Should man re-enact the ritual now and then with mortal bread and wine?

Is doing so not crucifying Jesus over and over again?

What Jesus did might be likened to the sprinkling of the blood of the Passover lamb on the lintel and doorposts in the enactment of the Passover in Egypt. Is that sprinkling re-enacted today in remembrance of the Passover in Egypt?

Jesus is the bread from heaven, and whoever chose to be His disciple is required to eat His flesh and drink His blood (John 6: 53, 58).

Thus it is His word alone that makes all disciples one body and one bread (1 Cor. 10:17, 21). This suggests the written word alone satisfies the required terms to mark the remembrance of Him. Any meal might do to make merry at the occasion.

The remembrance involves giving to fellow men that which has been received from the Lord concerning the gospel of Jesus crucified (1 Cor.

11:23–26). Feasting in a joyous atmosphere adds to the excitement of the remembrance but it is not the issue. The physical bread is manmade and it cannot have spiritual significance in the hand of sinful man. This assertion is based on the knowledge that what is ingested into the body will eventually go out of the body without any link to the heart, as to convey the message of the remembrance of Jesus (Mt. 15:11).

This suggests that it is a mental illusion to believe that brooding will make the unrighteous earthly bread and wine change to the real body and blood of Jesus respectively, and make it holy.

The moment Jesus became both poor and darkness

The exchange of rights between man and Jesus when He washed the feet of His disciples and at the last supper suggests the point of change. Jesus became both poor and darkness in addition to being the sins previously committed (2 Cor. 5:21a).

This implies that Jesus laid down His nature of God, who abhors sin before the rituals (John 10:17–18).

Now that Jesus has become the sins committed previously, God forsook Him (Mt. 27:46). So He was deprived of the wisdom of God. Following His arrest He was physically humiliated and deformed in shape like roasted meat, as it was foretold (Is. 52:14).

The deprivation of the wisdom of God made Jesus poor in heavenly riches, that through His poverty man might be rich with heavenly wisdom (Rom. 9:23–24).

God turned to man and appointed a second time for man to die

The exchange of sin and righteousness between man and Jesus set man free from sin and the captivity of Satan. It made him rich in the righteousness of God in Christ Jesus, and it reconciled man to God, who now turned to him and left Jesus alone.

God turned his love towards man, who was once lost but now found, in the likeness of the prodigal son (Lk. 15:20.)

But God turned his back on Jesus and forsook him (Mt. 27:46.)

Now man by proxy became the righteousness of God which was in Christ Jesus. As a result, God restored to man the options to make his own choice of either life and blessing, or death and curses with his free will (Deut. 30:19).

This put man back to the status of Adam without sin, at his creation in the beginning. It makes the choice which God has now given to man equivalent to His command to Adam in the beginning of what to eat and not to eat in the Garden of Eden. The implication of this conversely suggests that if a man chooses death and curses by denying Jesus, he will similarly surely die (Gen. 2:17).

This then becomes the second instance that God has appointed as a time for man to die, which will be after the judgment alluded to in the scripture (Heb. 9:27).

So there is work for man to do before judgment. This is the essence of the demand on man by the scripture to work out his salvation (Phil. 2:12).

It is worthy of note that the grace of God has not in any way waved aside this divine requirement of choice and the accompanying consequences (Rom. 8:1).

The crucifixion of Jesus on a tree (Deut. 21:23–24)

A disciple of Jesus (Judas Iscariot) betrayed Him. He was judged and condemned to death by crucifixion (Mt. 27:26). Then He was led away to be crucified.

On the way a certain Simon, who was coming out from the countryside, was compelled to carry His cross (Mk. 15:21). This was to suggest that Jesus suffered outside the gate in the countryside, that His blood might sanctify all the people (Heb. 13:12). Stoning was the customary way the Jews killed offenders after which the criminal was hung on a tree. So the Romans, who were experts in crucifixion, executed Jesus on a tree to satisfy the Jewish tradition of hanging criminals.

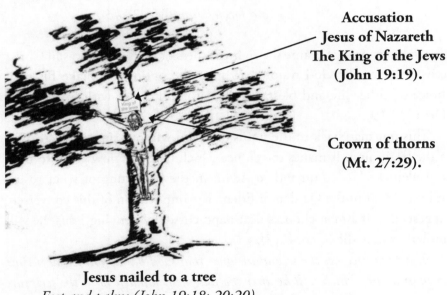

Accusation
Jesus of Nazareth
The King of the Jews
(John 19:19).

Crown of thorns
(Mt. 27:29).

Jesus nailed to a tree
Feet and palms (John 19:18; 20:20).

The significance of the crucifixion of Jesus outside the gate was to give an opportunity to all people to bear His reproach. This was to ensure that the blessing of the Spirit of glory and of God might be upon all men (1 Pet. 4:14).

It is this blessing by the work of divine instrument that is known as grace.

The intrinsic viciousness in crucifixion of Jesus

- The appearance of Jesus was marred like a roasted goat (Is. 52:14; Mt. 26:67).
- He bore our sins in His body, that we might live in righteousness of God in Him (1 Pet. 2:24). By this sacrifice Jesus broke down the former middle wall of separation between man and God on one hand, and between Israel and Gentiles on the other. This wall was originally set up by sin and the law in ordinances.

- However the sacrifice by Jesus abolished in His flesh the sin and law in ordinances, which was till then our enmity. Then He created in Himself one new man from the two – Israel and Gentiles – and He became our peace (Eph. 2:14–15).
- So He wiped out the accusation that was against us, rightly or wrongly, and nailed it to the cross (Col. 2:14).
- The cross crucified all to the world. It is a man who examines himself in this light that is fit to eat of the bread and drink of the cup of Jesus (Gal. 6:14).
- In which case, the cross reconciled to God in one body in Jesus all that have been crucified to the world (Eph. 2:13–16).
- After   the resurrection of Jesus, graves opened and many bodies of Patriarchs arose. The veil of the temple was torn in two from top to bottom (Mt. 27: 51–53).
- In spite of Jesus' inhumane treatment He pleaded with God on the cross to forgive man, declaring that he did not know what he was doing (Lk. 23:34).
- Furthermore, He showed His usual love when He forgave the sins of one thief who repented while crucified beside Him (Lk. 23:43).
- The hanging of Jesus on the tree redeemed man from the curse of the law as He became a curse for all that the Gentiles might receive Abraham's blessing and the promise of the Spirit through faith (Gal. 3:13–14).

The mystery of exchange in Jesus' burial and resurrection

1. The dead body of Jesus was laid in the tomb (MK. 15:46)

Entry to the tomb cut out of the rock where the body of Jesus was laid after crucifixion, and the door was secured with a stone across it.

Rocky platform where the tomb was carved out.

Stone rolled over the entrance to the tomb and sealed.

2. Resurrection: the body of Jesus rose from death on the third day (MK. 16:6)

'Resurrection' is the spirit of the gospel of salvation by grace (John 11:25).

**Lord Jesus Christ raised from the dead –
now fully God.**

Death could not hold His soul captive (Acts 2:24) unlike men who committed sin (Is. 51:5). The grave had now place for the body too (Ps.16:10).

3. Empty Tomb (Lk. 24:2–4, 12). This was verified and affirmed by Peter, et al.

Stone rolled aside from the entrace of the tomb.

Rocky platform

Open entrance to the tomb

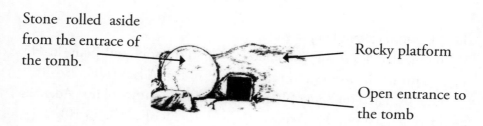

Jesus in death revived man after two days by conversion from darkness which is the forgetfulness of God to the citizenship of His Kingdom. On the third day He raised man to life (Hos. 6:2).

The resurrection of Jesus from the dead fulfilled the prophecy of Hosea that He will revive man (Hos. 6:2). It equally fulfilled the avowal of Jesus that He would raise the temple in three days if it was destroyed (John 2:19).

How was this done?

Let us examine what happened.

Recall that Jesus was the cohesion of spirit, soul and body in His human form. The form was in the likeness of first Adam (Phil. 2:7–8).

God prepared the soul of Jesus that was in the nature of first Adam as an offering for sin in the likeness of a lamb for sacrifice (Is. 53:10).

However, Jesus committed His spirit to the Father before He gave up the Ghost on the cross (Lk. 23:46). God gave Him the power to pick it up later (John 10:17–18).

All this was done that Jesus might fulfil the law of the principle of an eye for an eye and tooth for tooth in the revival of the sinful man once and forever (Ex. 21:24).

So in the death of Jesus, it was His body and soul alone that were destroyed.

In contrast, the spirit (Gal. 2:20) and body (Gal. 5:24) of the old man of former conduct (Rom. 6:6) were annihilated.

By the time Jesus was on earth man was living with the soul of the DNA of Adam. But God did not reckon with this soul because it manifested when Adam was already separated from Him (Gen. 5:3). It is believed that the DNA which made the soul to be the image and likeness of God is indestructible, and that it was frozen within him during the period.

This suggest that the soul of the DNA of God was only set free as slave to sin, that he might be revived in the spirit of the mind (Rom. 12:2) and be transformed by the Holy Spirit to the image of Christ (2 Cor. 3:18).

What has happened?

According to the scripture, the life of the soul is in the spirit (2 Cor. 3:6; Job 12:10). In the same vein, the life of the body is in the blood. God has given the blood to make atonement for the soul (Lev. 17:11).

So to cleanse the conscience of man and atone for his soul that his sins might be forgiven and his features revived (Lev. 24:20), the following happened:

- As previously examined, the exchange of rights between man and Jesus both at His washing of the feet of man and at the last supper made God to make Him who knew no sin to be sin (2 Cor. 5:21) which man has committed in the past (Rom. 3:25).
- Then the body of Jesus was sacrificed for God to create a new body in Him for man (Heb. 5:10). *This fulfilled the requirement of the law of blood for blood or body for body.*
- Similarly, the soul of Jesus which God has prepared specially for atonement was sacrificed in place of the soul of man (Is. 53:10).
- Thus the soul of man, which is the image of God and indestructible, was not annihilated.
- Rather, the soul of man was prepared for transformation into the image of Christ by the Holy Spirit (2 Cor. 3:18).
- As previously indicated, Jesus of the form of man laid down His spirit before He gave up the Ghost on the cross (Lk. 23:46). So the spirit of Jesus was not crucified.
- Rather, the spirit of man and the body of sin which had tied it up was destroyed in the death of Jesus, that he might be justified to receive another spirit from God (Rom. 6:6).

Then the death of the spirit of man was the justification for God to make the new creation spirit in Christ for man (Rom. 8:9).

All put together fulfilled the requirement of the law of life for life (Ex. 21:23).

As a result, God created a new man in Christ in place of the old man (Eph. 4:24). But the trade-in of the new man for the old man was preordained in milestone or to happen in phases as follows: first the spirit, followed by the soul and lastly the body at His coming (Phil. 3:21).

Now, therefore, when a man believes in Jesus, God will give to him the new creation spirit of Christ (Gal. 2:20) with the guarantee of a new body later (Rom. 8:11). Then the Holy Spirit will gradually transform the soul of whoever has received the new creation spirit to the image of Christ.

Analysis of "It is finished" (Jesus on the cross)

Background of this declaration by Jesus

God is sovereign and knows the end from the beginning of all things.

As a result, He knew there would be a future perversion of His works of creation. The creation was made perfect and upright in the beginning (Eccl. 7:29).

So God made a plan to redeem His creation from future perversion. At His appointed time, the need to execute the plan arose. But there was nobody in heaven, on earth or under the earth to do the job (Rev. 5:2–3).

It was at this crucial moment that the Lamb of God volunteered to take up the task (Rev. 5:5–7). This Lamb happened to be the Lion of the tribe of Judah and the Root of David. It was to execute the plan of God that He was born on earth in His first coming. He took the form of man and manifested on earth by the name of Jesus, the rod from the stem of Jesse and the branch which grew out of his roots in the tribe of Judah (Is. 11:1, 10).

However, the tribe of Judah was different from the tribe of Levites from which God chose to raise priests to serve at the earthly ark of tabernacle under the Law of Moses (Heb. 7:14).

In other words, Jesus was neither a priest of the law, nor a priest at all on earth (Heb. 9:24–25). He came to do the will of God. But it was not without drama.

The significance of "It is finished"

"It is finished" is an affirmation that the will of God has been successfully fulfilled with respect to the restoration of all previously perverse creation in human world.

A few of the innumerable rectified perversions in the past include the removal of the hitherto walls of separation (law of ordinances and sin) between God and man on one hand, and between the Israelites and the Gentiles on the other, making the two one (Eph. 2:15).

This was proved by the torn, three inch-thick veil of the temple, and its pulling apart from top to bottom (Mt. 27:51).

The pulling apart of the veil made the previously hidden sacred articles of the ark of tabernacle exposed to the view of all in the temple. This symbolised an unrestricted access for all men to God, and the placement of all on same pedestal. By the free access Jesus revealed God the Father to all.

Having free access to God is not for any man in darkness, which all men were prior to this event. But the free access is for all that Jesus gave birth to at the cross.

This happened when a Roman soldier pierced the side of Jesus to confirm that He was actually dead. Then water and blood gushed out to suggest birth. It was at this moment that the children of Jesus Christ who are now known as Christians were given birth to (John 19:34-35).

This was witnessed and testified to by the Spirit which is truth and by water and blood (1John 5:6, 8).

These are the three that bear witness of divine event on earth.

The ark of tabernacle, which was previously kept secret from all but the priest behind the veil (Heb. 9:4–5)

One of the two of the cherubim of glory that overshadowed the mercy seat.

Door to the Holy of Holy.

Ark of the covenant, overlaid on all sides with gold.

Inside: tablets of the covenant, Aaron's rod that budded, and Aaron's golden pot that held the manna and golden censer.

The veil torn from top to bottom, which pulled apart.

This suggests that Jesus is now the private Way to God for individual (John 14:6).

It is an indication that God has ceased to dwell in the temple made with hands (Acts 17:25). So the prophecy of Jeremiah that the ark will no longer be made or remembered in the time of grace was fulfilled (Jer. 3:16).

The exclamation signalled the end of the old way of life, in which man worshipped God by the sacrifice of the blood of animals (Is. 1:11). It marked the beginning of the new life of worship by faith (Is. 65:17).

Also, it marked the end of the priesthood of Levites in the tabernacle on earth, and the beginning of the priesthood of Christ Jesus in the tabernacle in heaven. As a result the hitherto shadow bond of Abraham to Melchizedek, who was the shadow of the priest of the heavenly tabernacle (Heb. 7:3), and of the Levite to the ark of tabernacle, which was on the other hand a shadow of the heavenly tabernacle, became a nullity (Heb. 9:11).

So the coming of Jesus, who is the substance of all holy things (Col. 2:17), of which Melchizedek was a shadow, elbowed out all previous dealings of man with Melchizedek because man was then shadow also (Heb. 7:11). This subsumed all formal relationships of the nature of shadow, including the 10% tithe by Abraham and the tithe of the Law into having faith in Jesus, the substance. It suggests an end to 10% tithing.

(A detailed commentary on Melchizedek, from *The Choice is Yours*, Article 44 and *Tithing* from the title *Return to God*, Chapter 41, can be read for free online at www.christthelordreign.com.)

The declaration signalled the forgiveness of sins and curses that were previously committed (Gal. 3:13; Col. 2:14), so all that man naively surrendered to Satan in Eden was restored to him.

This was the fulfilment of the promise of hope of eternal life to all families of the world through Abraham (Gen. 12:3c).

The new creation began with the resurrection of the body of Jesus Christ from death after the Holy Spirit gave life to the mortal body (Rom. 8:11). This suggests that Christ arose as a new, life-giving Spirit (1 Cor. 15:45b).

Thus the Jesus who was crucified in the form of a man was not the Jesus

Christ who arose from the dead as a Spirit being. This equally applies to whoever believed in Jesus (2 Cor. 5:16).

So whoever believes has to abide in Jesus Christ to produce fruit (Rom. 8:1a). This means that to backslide will take man back to the old beggarly life which God detests.

The declaration was the testimony of Jesus Christ that on earth He has glorified God the Father (John 10:28; 17:4). It signalled the response of God to the prayer for the kingdom of God to come to earth (Mt. 6:10). The accomplishment is much more than man can ever write.

Overall, 'it is finished' is indicative of 'Jesus as our Passover' sacrifice (1 Cor. 5:3). So whoever believes has equally passed over from sinful nature or darkness to the nature of light (Eph. 5:8) as a new creation in Christ (2 Cor. 5:17). It is this exchange of natures that the Lord's supper is designed to keep in remembrance of Jesus as the author and be a wothy Partaker. This Christianity is a daily lifestyle of spirit nature producing the fruit of the Spirit (Gal. 5:22-23). Now it is the Lord that puts men in position of specific authority (Eph. 4:11; 1 Cor. 12:5) having been given in heaven and on earth (Mt. 28:18; Eph. 1:22).

The behaviours which glorify God

Judas Iscariot betrayed Jesus, which coupled with his envy and greed, suggests that he did not believe in Him. So his remorse was predicated upon regret for making unprofitable bargain, losing face with people, and losing the position of keeping the purse which together make the repentance the sorrow of the world. This made the denial of Jesus by apostle Peter different from the betrayer by Judas.

However, his betrayal inadvertently first made Jesus to be glorified. Then it paved the way for Jesus to glorify God the Father (John 13:31).

With respect to man, the way to glorify God is to obey the word and submit to Him, which is his faith in action (Ps. 103:20; 1 Thes. 4:1–4).

The 'doing' is to obey the intrinsic voice of the spirit of faith, which may be by a hunch or desire. It is different from doing the requirement of the law. It is upon this that the daily living grace of man is based.

This suggests that it would be a misreading of the scriptures to believe that under the gospel of grace, man is not required to do anything, or that any wrongdoing after man has once believed is covered by grace.

When Jesus was faced with the task of executing the final plan of God, He first prayed to the Father to let the cup to pass away if it were possible.

But God did not grant His prayer which suggests that the task was for Jesus to glorify Him (John 17:1-8).

Then He succumbed to let the will of God be done (Mt. 26:42).

It suggests that to backslide without repenting is to deny glorifying God with the opportunity Christ has given to man.

Comparing 'new creation man' and 'earthly man'

Comparing Jesus born in the form of man, and Lord Jesus, who is fully Spirit

Before Cruxifixion
Jesus with human body
(1 Cor. 15:40b)

Christ the Lord

Jesus Christ human nature

Jesus was born to live in the likeness of man. He had spirit, soul and body like Adam (Phil. 2:6–7). Jesus also had God's nature at the same time.

In death He lost His soul of the likeness of Adam to make atonement and save all souls from the sins man committed (Is. 53:10).

This Jesus could only enter a confined place through an entrance.

Post Ressurection

After Jesus arose His form became Spirit entirely (2 Cor. 5:16). The earthly body of flesh changed to a divine form.

Proof is His ability to enter or leave a confined space without a doorway, and to ascend and descend at will. Now He has overcome death. So He is dead to the world by the cross (John 16:33).

Comparing 'man in and of the world' and 'man in but not of the world'

The believer is in but not of the world, as compared to the unbeliever who is in and of the world (John 17: 11, 14).

However, Jesus died for the sins committed by all, and He was equally raised for all by proxy. So all men were united together in the likeness of His death, and all shall similarly be so in His resurrection (Rom. 6:4–5).

The sinful man united with Jesus in the likeness of His death.

The man raised in the likeness of resurrected Christ the Lord.

The sinful man is required to believe in Jesus to profit from His atonement (John 3:16).

Until he believes, his spirit shall not be replaced by the new. That will lead him to remain dead to righteousness of God. He will still be faced with fears of death, filled with worries, doubt, have double mind and desires for earthly things, etc.

This is former sinful man who has believed in Jesus that he was in bond with Him in death and resurrection. Now God has given him the spirit of Christ, made righteous and holy (Eph. 4:24). Though still in his old body, the Holy Spirit is now transforming his soul into the image of Christ (2 Cor. 3:18).

The Holy Spirit shall lastly give life to his mortal body (Rom. 8:11). Now he is regarded as spirit like Christ (2 Cor. 5:16). So he daily exudes the fruit of the spirit (Gal. 5:22–23).

Chapter Sixteen

The Last Two Commands

Wisdom teaches that the events of crucifixion and later resurrection paint a picture of two different personalities of Jesus Christ, namely:

The Jesus who lived on earth in the likeness of man (Phil. 2:6–7). He was falsely accused, and finally killed and buried (Rom. 6: 4a). This is the Child that was born by Mary, and the Son that was given by God (Is. 9:6). At the twilight of His mission He commanded man through His disciples to keep Him in remembrance by the last supper which He had with them (Lk. 22:20). This was the first of the two last commands in the world whose extinction is imminent.

Three days after the burial of Jesus, another Jesus Christ the Lord arose, with the body of the buried Jesus but changed to a different physiology by the power of the Holy Spirit (Rom. 6:4b). This divine Jesus Christ gave another last command to man to *Go into the world and make disciples of all nations*. It is this command that man has labelled the 'Great Commission' (Mt. 28:19–20).

The command simply calls for a purposeful evangelism by every believer in Jesus Christ. Now a believer is to regard himself to be a new creation spirit like the Lord Jesus (2 Cor. 5:16). Then live by faith (Ps. 1:1–3), and exude the fruit of the Spirit as a daily lifestyle (Gal. 5:22–23).

Wisdom further teaches that the last two commands are seamless. However the first, which was made when both man and Jesus were in the form of man, is now to fit into the second, which was made when both are now regarded according to the spirit. In other words, the first, which was ritual in practice under the law, has now rolled over into the heavenly form under grace. The rollover suggests the replacement of the earthly elements before the crucifixion with Devine elements because the natural man who has believed has also changed to the spirit nature (2Cor. 5:16). Natural man and things are shadows and perishing unlike the believer and Devine elements (2Cor. 4:16). This suggests the essence of the rollover from shadow to everlasting elements (John 6:31, 49).

An example of a perishing item in the ritual of last supper is material bread but the corresponding substance which exists forever is the word of God which is the bread from heaven (Rev. 2:17, John 6:27).

Similar rollovers abound in the scriptures for our learning, even though this understanding might have been hidden from man for centuries. However they are scriptures which man deals with from time to time.

Command by Jesus as a man is now fulfilled according to the Spirit

Instances of rollover of the earthly into the divine command

A few examples of the rollover of old practices under the law into a different mode in the gospel of grace might suffice for our understanding.

The sticky point in this principle of rollover is that the same Physiology of man appears to be responsible on both sides. But this is not so. Once a man believes he is a changed being and this should reflect in his conduct.

While some practices decreased and gradually faded out, others rolled over and became embedded into new practices.1. Worship by sacrifice of animals at the altar under the law rolled over to *worship by faith in spirit and truth* under grace (John 17:14, 16). 2. In this case, the old ceased to be relevant. 3. Under the law, touching the wings 0r helm of Jewish garment will bring healing according to prophecy (Mal. 4:2). 4. But this belief rolled over to *faith* in the gospel of grace. As a result, the woman with the issue of blood was not healed due to the old belief but was healed by her faith in Jesus. The testimony of this is thamany other people touched the wings of Jesus' garment by either accident, or deliberately and were not healed (Lk. 8:46).5. But she was healed by her faith in Jesus, which suggests that the healing power of the wings has rolled over to faith in Jesus (Lk. 8:48).

6 Under the law, God had a portion of the tithing to the Levite who rendered service to Him as their inheritance (Num. 18:20–21).Bur God gave His portion to the priest (Num. 18:26).

Tithe was not to be transferred between tribes because it was an inheritance (Num. 36:9).

Under faith, the tithing rolled over to *giving services to the jailed, the widowed, the fatherless, the naked, the hungry, etc.* God sees these as though done to Him (Mt. 25:40). This suggests that tithing is not relevant in the gospel of grace.

7. Under the law fasting was mainly on abstinence from food, drink and sex. But under faith, fasting rolled over to a *daily lifestyle* of showing love and mercy to fellow men, helping the widowed and fatherless, seeking freedom for the oppressed, undoing heavy burdens, sharing generously as desired in the heart, and so on (Is. 58:6–7).

It is in a similar way, the last command of "Do this in remembrance of Me" has rolled over from ritual with material things to the last command of *"Go into the world and make disciples of all nations"*, which is done with the word of God, the true bread from heaven, and is known as the Great Commission.

The two commands were made by Jesus to the same man of darkness (the spirit and outward parts do not know God) in the world of darkness.

When Jesus gave the first command He was known according to the form of a fully earthly man, although He was also fully God in the world of darkness.

By the second command, Jesus has become fully God alone in the realm of light, having sacrificed the earthly man that He was previously to save man (Is. 53:10).

Now the man who has believed has the spirit in light, but his outward being is in darkness. This suggests that to be in same realm with Christ there is need to rollover the 'remembrance of Me' to the 'Great Commission'. This is because it is believed that it is a double standard to perform the ritual under the law in darkness and combine it with the gospel of grace in light. Such might be tantamount to being lukewarm, which the scripture has discredited (Rev. 3:16). Now the man raised from the dead is regarded according to the spirit, unlike the man before crucifixion.

The amalgamation of the two commands will suggest that the earthly 'bread and wine', which under the law represented the body and blood of Jesus, have rolled over to the word of God and meditating on it These represent His 'flesh and blood' respectively under grace (John 6:55–58).

This suggests the requirement of remembrance is to feed on the word of God, and at the same time ponder on Jesus hanging on the cross of Calvary (1Cor. 10:17; 11:23-26).

According to scripture activities of earthly nature such as use of material bread and wine is carnal. Earthly bread and wine are for merry making during remembrance. Sincerely, there is no depth of thought of man which will make material bread and wine assume the forms of the real body and blood of Jesus respectively. To set mind on things above and on things on earth is in the likeness of sitting on the fence. Both the Lord Jesus Christ and the man who believed are now of the same new spirit nature, and of one body (2 Cor. 5:16).

Therefore, both now feed on and drink the same word of God as the common bread of all believers as one body (1 Cor. 10:17; Deut. 8:3).

Looking back to the beggarly life under the law makes the practice of the last supper non-uniform, which is against the spirit of remembrance (1 Cor. 10:16–17). Rather, rely on the word as the bread and ponder on the event of the crucifixion as the blood, with thanksgiving to God for His forgiveness of the sins committed previously (Rom. 3:25).

However, the ritual of bread and wine of material things represents the feasting which is necessary in the occasion of last supper. It is taken in a worthy manner when all attention is set on Jesus hanging from the cross, and in addition ruminates on His suffering for you while partaking in discussion and the feast. It is believed that this is how to proclaim the death of the Lord (1 Cor. 11:26).

To be absentminded of the passion of Jesus while taking part in the last supper is an unworthy manner of participation, and the scripture frowns at it (1 Cor.11:27–29).

Chapter Seventeen

The Great Forgiveness by Grace

The background

The idea and execution of the great forgiveness of the sins which were committed in the past were exclusively of God (Rom. 3:25). The exercise was to fulfil the preordained choice of God which He made before the foundation of the world to give life back to man whenever he lost it (Eph. 1:4), and the promise He made to Abraham (Lk. 1:70-75; Acts 3:25).

The instrument by which God executed this, precisely for the sake of His name only, is what is known as grace. *This suggest that grace is not a matter of pity, or a favour to man.* Rather, it is a godly operation for a divine purpose (Rom. 8:29).

This was done with the instrument of governance in the kingdom of God (1 Pet. 4:14). Detailed information on grace shall be given in a later chapter in this book.

At the last supper with the disciples, the imminent giving of grace to man through Jesus (John 1: 17) was demonstrated and celebrated. During the occasion, Jesus gave his body and blood, which He symbolised with bread and wine respectively, to man, that he might become the righteousness of God in Christ, through faith (2 Cor. 5:21).

This set forth the great forgiveness through the redemption that is in Christ Jesus. God made Him to shed His blood to pave way for the justification for man, through faith, to profit from the annulment of all the iniquity and transgressions and sins which man had committed in the past (Rom. 3:25).

It made everybody a beneficiary of the forgiveness of previous sins, which made the forgiveness common to all, irrespective of belief (Jude 3a).

The significance of this is that the forgiveness by grace put all persons on the same clean state and starting line to embark on their individual race of life by faith, as a new person that has never committed sin (Heb.12:1–2; 1 Cor.9:24).

Analysis of David's prophecy on the great forgiveness

King David saw the vision of this 'great forgiveness by grace' from far off, and so wrote of *the Blessedness of the man to whom God imputes righteousness apart from works (Rom.4:6)*. This suggests that the man to whom David referred is the believer in Jesus Christ whose previous sins have been forgiven him (Acts 14:16).

It was for the sake of Israel alone that King David wrote: *Blessed are those whose lawless deeds are forgiven, and whose sins are covered (Rom. 4:7)*.

It will be recalled that it was to Israel alone that God gave the law, which gave her some form of relationship with Him. The law reigned supreme in Israel until after the passion of Jesus, so to speak.

The law gave privilege to Israel. When Israel sinned she would make sacrifice to God, and as a result He would forgive her lawless deeds and cover the sins she committed against herself and the law, by reason of His favour and mercy. This is what made the assertion of David most apt to Israel alone.

Then, for the sake of the Gentiles alone, King David wrote: *Blessed is the man to whom the Lord shall not impute sin.*

The Gentile lived in lawlessness from the onset till the passion of Jesus, but God ignored him and did not impute to him the sin he committed (Rom. 5:13). This allowed the Gentile to be the first to enjoy the proclamation of King David.

However, by the atonement of Jesus God created one man from the two. Then this man, when he believes in Jesus, becomes the man to whom God imputes righteousness apart from works (Eph. 2:15). As a result, he becomes a beneficiary of the pronouncement of David on the proviso that he remains steadfast in Christ.

The foregoing suggests that the scriptures ascribed to David and quoted along are specific to sins committed in the past and they do not cover or envisage sins that might be committed in the present and future.

It means that every sin that might be committed presently or in the future has to be confessed with repentance (Acts 17:30).

The role of Holy Spirit in the great forgiveness of sins

Two hitherto unknown significant things happened in sequence after the risen Jesus Christ reconnected with His disciples: the Lord Jesus gave the Holy Spirit, and He baptised man with the Holy Spirit.

In the first place Christ gave to His disciples who have believed in Him the Holy Spirit and commision them to make disciples of all nations of the world in a similar manner to that in which the Father sent Him. This is the Spirit of Christ, which God now gives to whoever believes in Jesus to live for Him and no longer for self (Gal. 2:20). He additionally accorded them the right to forgive or retain the sins of anyone with the assurance that heaven shall respond in concurrence (John 20: 22–23).

Consequently, Jesus Christ expected them to take up the duty of carrying forward the good news of the kingdom of God and His resurrection. However, a man may still backslide irrespective of this new creation Spirit in him because of the antics of the spirit of sin which still dwells in member of the flesh, represented by the self-will nature in man (Rom. 7:20).

This suggests that a limitless number of spirits can dwell in man. Therefore, the more expressive schemer and dominant spirit might influence the direction of man if he is not committed to the gospel of Jesus crucified. Apostle Peter strikes an example of one misdirected by the spirit of sin when he abandoned the course of the ministry of Jesus to go fishing again, even after His resurrection (John 21:3).

Secondly, Christ baptised man on the day of Pentecost with the Holy Spirit. *This is the baptism with the Holy Spirit and fire by Jesus Christ which John spoke of (Lk. 3:16).* The disciples, including the new replacement for the son of prediction, which is the vessel created by God for destruction, and others totalling 120 souls, gathered in the upper room. They were jointly in prayer and supplication. Suddenly a sound came from heaven like a rushing, mighty wind. Then it settled like a divided tongues as of fire or the distributaries of a river upon the twelve disciples whom Christ earlier chose, and whom He also instructed after His resurrection to wait for power or the promise of the Father (Acts 1: 2, 4, 8).

The track record of Jesus suggests that the Holy Spirit did not settle on the rest of the people present, even though they were worthy, committed souls (Rev. 3:4). The promise was to the chosen disciples alone, and what He said, He will do, because the Lord is not the God of confusion.

Then each spoke in the unfamiliar but discernible tongues of the nations of the world, and the spread of the church of Christ took root on earth (Acts 2:2–4).

The twelve disciples

Holy Spirit (power) in the likeness of fire perched upon the disciples.

Peter, James, John, Andrew, Philip, Thomas, Bartholomew, Matthew, James the son of Alphae'us, Simon the Zealot, Judas the son of James, and Matthias.

The Holy Spirit's power energised them and from then on spoke boldly in defence of the word of God. They all continued in one accord to preach and teach the gospel of Jesus.

It will be recalled that the gospel was born when a soldier pierced the side of Jesus on the cross with a spear, and blood and water came out (John 19:34). But it was on the day of Pentecost that the gospel of grace became known as the only effective way to know the truth and be made free (Acts 2:22–24).

Chapter Eighteen

The Divine Virtue of a Christ like Life

Every descendant of Adam is born on earth with dull life of iniquity (Ps. 51:5).

However, man is awakened to overcome the defect when the core value of heavenly life, by the knowledge of God, manifests in him (Rom. 13:11–14). This will make man a person of the fibre of divine virtue. The beatitudes analysis:

Sinful man

Persecuted for righteousness' sake, and falsely for the sake of Jesus: It is to have mind set on heaven and be unwilling to deny Christ and compromise, and as a result become target of hate (1 Pet. 3:17).

Peacemaker: have a penchant to sacrifice self-interest willingly for others with good conscience, and to live by the truth (1 Pet. 3:16).

Pure in heart: honest, just and fast by sacrificial love as shown in Chapter 11 (1 Cor.13:12).

Merciful: a cheerful giver with a considerate heart (2 Cor.9:7).

Mourn: To have a mind to show anguish for foolish conduct and lack of knowledge of God by men (John 11:33–35; 2 Cor.7:7–10).

Hunger and thirst for righteousness: persuade self not to make a sacrifice of the law, but choose to live a humble life as per the word of God and seek to exude the fruit of the Spirit daily, even in famine (Lk. 1:38; Amos 8:11).

Meek: To be meek is to constrain use of advantage of anything to the detriment of others, under any situation (John 19:11; 1Sam. 24:8–11).

Nothing is new on earth – all regenerate (Eccl. 1:4–7)

Civilisation merely opens what has been hidden

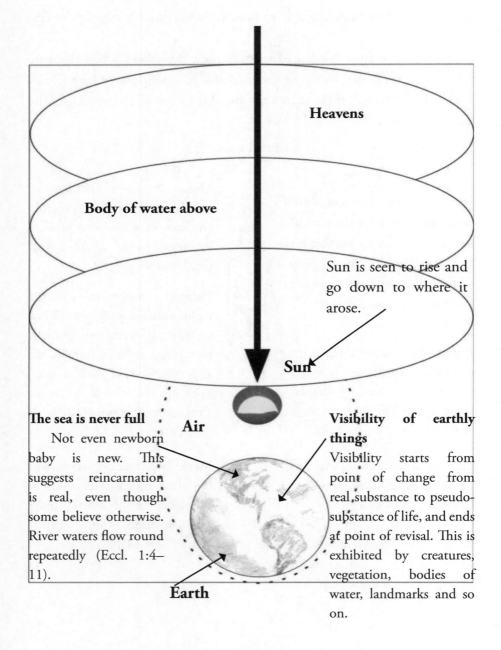

Heavens

Body of water above

Sun is seen to rise and go down to where it arose.

Sun

The sea is never full

Not even newborn baby is new. This suggests reincarnation is real, even though some believe otherwise. River waters flow round repeatedly (Eccl. 1:4–11).

Air

Visibility of earthly things

Visibility starts from point of change from real substance to pseudo-substance of life, and ends at point of revisal. This is exhibited by creatures, vegetation, bodies of water, landmarks and so on.

Earth

The lessons from the recycling of the creation of God

There is nothing visible on earth that is excluded from the cycle of going and coming (Heb. 11:3; 2 Cor.4:18).

The case of man is even more decisive. This is because he is God, or a chip of the rock which is the Lord. God pulled him out from Himself once (Gen. 1:26–27). Therefore he has to be regenerated in his choice of life to get an opportunity to attain perfection. This programme is only available through life on earth (2 Cor. 3:18).

This suggests that reincarnation of man is real. Jesus clearly stated that the prophecy that Elijah would come first before the Saviour was fulfilled. Implying that John the Baptist came in the spirit of Elijah (Mk. 9:11–13; Lk.1:17).

So the misreading of the scriptures by man will not change what is.

Until man is made perfect or condemned through his own choice he will not have the qualification to ascend to eternity (Reference: page 1 of Chapter 1). It is the desire of God not to see anybody perish that is responsible for the longsuffering of God (2 Pet. 3:9).

Let God who is righteous be true, but every man who is unrighteous a liar (Rom. 3:4).

The birth and death phenomena happen only in the world of time, which is where we now live according to available knowledge, and in it every host is toiling. Outside it is eternal and only those already adjudged either righteous or condemned will live permanently in eternity, either at rest or in torment respectively, which will take place on the day of judgment (Reference: Chapter 38B).

It is only on earth that there is opportunity to make the right choice of life. Until the door which Christ has opened is closed for judgment, all visible things shall continue to appear and exist for a time, then disappear and later reappear, and repeat the cycle over and over again as appointed by God (Eccl. 1:9–11).

This suggests why the gathering and collecting of earthly things which will perish with time is vanity. It boils down to lack of divine knowledge. As a result men resort to doing things their own way or according to scholarship or establishment.

Chapter Nineteen

Christianity is Stewardship for God or Seeking The Kingdom of God by Imitating Jesus

(So Christianity is a loose coinage for Discipleship)

In practice it is to live a life of service as a Steward who obeys the word of God. The scriptures describe the man whom Jesus called to follow Him a disciple.

A disciple is he who follows Jesus with dedication, learns from Him, and imitates the Master in all aspects of life (1 Cor. 11:1). This oddness of their life led observers in Antioch to nickname them Christians (Acts 11:26). The nickname has since become the identity of the faith. But Christianity has since then meant just a label, and not what the disciple of Christ represents. So today many regard Christianity as a 'relationship' with God. This classification suggests a loose bond between man and God of which either partner can quit at any time when it is so desired without consequences. This is in contrast with the duty of a warden, which God made man to be at creation (Gen 2:5. 15). Today adherents of the faith follow personalities or establishments first before the Master, against the advice of the scripture (Mt. 23:10). Thus Jesus has become a second fiddle in the practice of Christianity. Nobody seems to care about the scripture, which warns against thinking of oneself more than what he really is (Rom. 12:3).

God created man for Himself (Col. 1:16) to please Him (Eph. 1:5; Phil. 2:13) and give Him glory (Is.43:7). It was to achieve this purpose that He put him in Eden to manage and to be legally responsible for all things in the kingdom (Gen. 2:5c; 2:15). This made man a warden to provide service, and so worship God by it. *It is the practice that has been labelled religion. The aim of giving life back to man remains the same today.* When man disobeyed God He drove him out of Eden. As a result his service and worship ceased. Then man started to seek God. This led him to invent the medium of the shrine in an attempt to find 'God'. But his efforts misdirected him to change the glory of God to an image made like corruptible mammals and birds, and the works of his hands (Rom. 1:23). *As a result, man turned to please Deity, which he believed to be God, and serviced and worshipped it through perverse form or flip side of perfect service or religion.* This is how religion became the medium to please either God or Satan. Afterwards, God found Abraham, who built the first altar to make sacrifice to God (Gen. 12:7). Other altars were made to make sacrifice to God (Gen. 22:9–10).

Later, the Law of Moses was given. Then God commanded Moses to make a permanent altar to worship Him. Then the ark of tabernacle was made after the pattern of the tabernacle in heaven (Ex. 25:40).

In all worship, *relationship* is the common thread between man and whatever he serves. So to label any faith as a relationship suggests a discredit to the faith. *Therefore, to label Christianity as a relationship is a way to demean God either inadvertently or deceitfully.* This is because it degrades the Creator to a position of equality with His creatures, which unbelievers worship as their gods and have common relationships with.

What has changed?

The atonement of Jesus re-engineered the old pattern to please God. So for a disciple the duty remains same, and as a steward he serves and worships by means of religion, as seen previously.

But this religion of the body of Christ has transformed into what the scripture tagged as '*pure and undefiled religion*' (James 1:27).

It is this peculiarity of the religion of Christianity (discipleship) that has now sets it apart from other religions of men around the world.

The mode of worship of God in this pure and undefiled religion of Christianity is to do service to fellow men which the scriptures regard as service to God in addition to studying the word with prayers and supplications. This is the true worship of God whom we do not see (1 John 4:20).

The fellow men could be the widowed, the fatherless, the hungry, the prisoner, the oppressed, those in service of God, and so on (Mt. 25:40).

The foregoing behaviour is to be the lifestyle of the Christian who is truly the disciple of Christ as a demonstration of the love of God according to the scriptures (John 13:34–35). It alludes to both faith in God (Heb. 11:6) and worship in spirit and truth (John 4:24).

In respect of relationship, God made man in a similar manner to the potter who fingers the clay. Now that man is a disciple of Christ, he remains like clay and a lesser god to the greater God the Father, who is like the potter (Rom. 9:20–24).

So the true relationship between Christianity and God is like that between the clay and potter respectively. *Hence Christianity is stewardship and not relationship.*

Stewardship is first the affairs of the heart where God who looks at the heart is the judge of individual's standing with Him, but is next shown outwardly to win souls for Christ that God might be glorified (1 Sam. 16:7).

God reveals to the good steward by His Spirit the things which might keep his soul from perishing in dreams and vision (Job 33:15–18; John 15:15).

The good steward is the clay which yeilds to the potter. Yielding leads to fellowship which is the root of the relationship that exists between man and God. Its purpose is for man to be Priest to serve God (1 Rev. 1:56). Thus, Adam's stewardship or service was the birth or origin of religion in Eden. Therefore, religion is the practical demonstration of allegiance of man, as clay, to the potter, who is God in the case of Christianity. In Eden, Adam provided this service by tending the garden which is a metpahor for worship. After Adam sinned, the process of service flipped over to religion under the law.

Then man began his service to gods and later to God by the Jews alone through the sacrifice on the altar of earth (Ex. 20:24). But under grace God commanded light to shine in the dark heart of man to beam the knowledge of His glory in the face of Christ (2 Cor. 4:6).

Recounting, self is what man sees when le looks at a mirror. As man is God's image and likeness and thus His glory he sees himself in the face of Christ (Gen. 1:26:27). So by seeing the glory of God in the face of Christ, God called man into the fellowship of Chirst (1 Cor. 1:9). It is this fellowship that will make man to abide in Christ (John 15:4) as a Kingdom and priest to offer sacrifice to God (1 Pet. 2:5, 9). So man is to worship God (1 Cor. 1:5) in the likeness of the service by upright Adam in Eden.

Thus, Christianity is not relationsip but the demonstation of allegiance by man as lesser being to God who is the great being. This service suggests it is done by pure and undefiled religion (James 1:27).

Chapter Twenty

Vision of the Grace of God

Examination of grace

Many regard grace as unmerited favour. It is also said that *past, present and future* sins have been forgiven. How true is this? Let us examine the scriptures. Grace came through Jesus (John 1:17). *Without ambiguity, the scripture is clear that God forgave man of only the sins that were committed previously (Rom. 3:25).*

This suggests that the entire human race has been saved by grace once (Eph. 2:8). This is the common salvation (Jude 3a) by grace. It is this man to whom God will not impute sin whenever he believes and abides in Jesus thereafter, going by King David's prophecy (Rom. 4:8). In which case, he does not sin because of the seed of God in him and has been born of God (John 3:9).

All sins by Israel and the lawless deeds by Gentiles prior to the sacrifice by Jesus were forgiven and forgotten by God to fulfil prophecy (Is. 43:25; Rom. 4:7). God promised not to remember them again (Heb. 8:12; Heb. 10:17). *All these texts on forgiveness will survive only in the context of the common salvation.* No man will ever be punished or judged on account of the sins for which Jesus suffered, or be alienated from God because of them. This suggests that once a man believes, he is obliged to abide in Christ (Mk. 8:34; John 15:4).

So it does not mean that the 'now and future' sins have been forgiven. Rather, it puts burden on man not to look back to sin. *If a blind man in the likeness of Abram at the time God called him believes, God will impute his belief to him for righteousness, apart from his works (Rom. 4:6).* Then God will next give the gift of Spirit of faith to the man (Ron. 4:5). This gift of faith is what assists man to have his own divine faith and to know that He is God.

To the man who has faith, God will give the new heart and new Spirit made in holiness and righteousness (Eph. 4:24).

Then the Holy Spirit will seal the Spirit to preserve the virtue (Eph. 1:13). This is the born-again man (Spirit alone) who does not sin (1 John 3:9).

The role of spirit in man, as seen earlier, suggests that the entire man is to walk by faith in line with the new Spirit (Rom. 8:1, 4; 1 Tim. 6:1) to please God (Heb. 11:6). But the weakness of the body and soul in the interim makes it a challenge.

Balancing the above expectation and reality further shows that the present and future sins have not been forgiven. Can this righteousness be reversed? *Yes.*

The prophecy which says that if a man who once received righteousness happens to backslide and will not repent, he will die like Adam, says so (Ezek. 18:24). So the quote 'that *all died in Adam*' is not parallel to the quote '*that all might live in Christ*'. Now man has a choice to make (Deut. 30:19) and a command to work out own salvation to obey (Phil. 2:12). A wrong choice or partiality, which God hates (James 2:1, 4), will hurt him. The scripture made it known that the guilty and the backslider will not enter the kingdom (Gal. 5:19–21).

So, man shall account for present and future sins on day of the Lord (2 Cor. 5:10). Meanwhile God sees only the new creation spirit which He gave to who believed in the form of Christ. God does not see the body and soul who is the real man until they are righteous and Holy. Now the soul is to work out his own salvation through the rewashing by the word by Holy Spirit and abide in Christ (2 Cor. 3:18; John 15:5).

Not understanding this suggests the thinking that now God sees entire believer's components as Christ and so he cannot be unrighteous agian.

In that case, what then is truly the grace of God?

Ask the Holy Spirit (1 Cor. 2:13).

However let us examine what the grace of God really represents from the next page.

Illustration: Back end happenings in mans' heart.

Heaven
Shower of grace

Instrument of governance in Kingdom of God includes

love, justice, peace, joy, righteousness, etc. This is how God works in man to work out own Salvation (Phil. 2:13-13).

Similar instrument in human governance includes: police, army, etc.

The plane of stars

Represents the kingdom of God within man and is formed in the heart by imprints made by divine tools of governance as intervention in man's life by Christ. The imprint of love saved all men (John 3:16; Eph. 2:8) – refer table ahead. It is the imprint in heart that is decoded to be grace outwardly (1 Pet 4:14).

Two spiritual kingdoms exist in the heart of every man:

1. Kingdom of iniquity and sins (dark plane).
2. Kingdom of God (plane of stars; Lk. 17:21).

The dark plane

represents the kingdom of darkness of iniquity and sins into which man is born (Ps. 51:5), he being darkness too (Eph. 5:8).

Remarks on the illustration

Truth, which is (the life of) the word of God (John 17:17), is what conveys divine virtues. The features of divine virtues are the instruments of governance in heaven.

They are poured out of heaven to make imprints which form the kingdom of God within man. *Imprints signify the intervention of Christ in man's situation.* This is the ongoing back end activity of grace.

It is the imprint that the scripture has decoded in the front end, or outwardly, as the grace of God.

Love is the prime instrument of governance, and its imprint is the bedrock of the kingdom of God within man (Lk. 17:21). In any situation of man an apt imprint of grace might appear to lend a hand.

The plane of darkness of iniquity and sin into which man is born and lives lies below the bedrock plane, indicated with stars.

It is from the kingdom of darkness that a man of faith might through Christ access the kingdom of God within him, to obtain mercy and find grace to aid in times of need (Heb. 4:16).

In other words, man requires faith to ascend to stand in grace, and the aftermath is the opportunity to rejoice in hope of the glory of God (Rom. 5:2).

To stand in grace grants man the benefit of the reign of Christ, or His governance.

Hence faith is the victory that has overcome the world (1 John 5:4). So faith, which actually means to surrender to the word of God, is all that man requires to overcome the world.

Explanation of how grace helps man

The healing of the woman with the issue of blood is a good example of how grace helps man. The account suggests that she believed a hunch, which came from the Spirit of faith, that touching the hem of the robe of Jesus would heal her. Then she surrendered to the voice, which is the practical way to show faith. So she obeyed the intrinsic work in the voice by secretly touching the hem of the robe of Jesus Christ (Mk. 5:30).

As expected, she was healed by the grace of God. Jesus equally noticed that power left Him, which suggests that grace is a result of back end activity as shown previously.

In other words, that Jesus felt some power leave Him suggests that grace is caused by some sort of operation by a certain force in the kingdom of God. That certain force is the action of instrument of governance in the kingdom.

Governance in the kingdom is the description of the reign of Christ.

So grace is the expression on earth of the imprint made by the intervening force of the reign of Christ in the kingdom of God within man.

That is to say that, the intervening power of the reign of Christ first makes a divine imprint in the kingdom of God within man.

Then the imprint is decoded in the dark spirit realm of iniquity and sin in man's heart (Ps. 51:5), and made known to the outward senses as grace.

To go back to the woman – she was darkness and lived in the plane of darkness (Eph. 5:8). But her faith lifted her up to the plane of grace. Then she found grace to help in her need, and she was healed (Heb. 4:16).

The declaration by Jesus that the woman's faith healed her testified to the role of faith in the matters of grace (Mk. 5:34).

To recap, the imprint which is made in the kingdom of God within man is known on earth as grace. Every imprint is made by an intervening power from heaven and is known as the instrument of governance in the reign of Christ.

The benefit of grace is spiritual in form. It is in the likeness of the wind, which is neither seen nor touchable but can be made conscious of by feeling or hearing.

What this means is that any tangible benefit derived from inhumanly impossible circumstances or unexpected sources is not a result of grace. Rather, such benefit is as a result of favour.

The proof that grace is the imprint of the reign of Christ

Let us consider two scenarios:

1. It is the grace of God alone which enables man to endure and bear and hope and believe all things. These are basics of love (1 Cor. 13:7).
   i. An example is the man who cannot exercise self-control so as not to avenge injustices such as reproaches, slaps, persecution and insults unless by grace of God (1 Pet. 3:14).
2. On the other hand, to face reproach and still be calm is a sign of the presence of the Spirit of glory, and of God acting upon the victim (1 Pet. 4:14).

Now harmonise the two scenarios and it will suggests that the Spirit of glory and of God upon man is a description of the grace of God upon man. As it has been previously shown, grace is a label, or decoding, of the *imprint* by instrument of divine governance.

But it was explained previously an imprint is the foot print made by instrument of reign of Spirit of glory, and of God.

Now Jesus Christ is the glory of God, and He is also the express nature of God (Heb. 1:3). This suggests that the action of the Spirit of glory and of God is a description of the stewardship of Jesus Christ.

But the stewardship depicts the reign of the Lord Jesus Christ. Therefore, it means that *grace is the imprint of the reign of Jesus Christ* upon a given situation. (Quod erat demonstrandum)

Table of analysis

Without doubt, favour of God is unmerited.

What then can be said of grace? Could it be a doubly unmerited favour?

Certainly that will sound unknowledgeable.

This suggests, therefore, that to label grace as unmerited favour denies the truth. One benefit of this new reading is that grace will constantly remind man of the presence of the Lord Jesus Christ in our heart – the plane of stars in the previous illustration.

The table of grace

The purpose of grace is that all of mankind might become the righteousness of God in Christ (2 Cor. 5:21).

Heaven	Kingdom of God within man (Lk. 17:21)	Life on earth
Wisdom from God in Christ for man (1 Cor. 1:30)	*Imprint of reign of Christ (plane of stars)*	*Grace (decoding of the imprint of the reign of Christ)*
Christ is the storehouse of God for all his glorious things of honour. Each item is instrument of governance which is hung on jeus as a niche on a wall to hold all treasures of the home (Is. 22:22-24)	Expression of godly perspectives	Fulfilment of the promise of heavenly nature: …in you all the families of the earth shall be blessed (Gen. 12:3b). Prior to advent of Jesus, God thrust grace onto Noah to save human race from annihilation (Gen. 6:8), that the promise of God might be fulfilled by, and in, Jesus (John 3:16). Unlike Noah, grace is personified in Christ. It gets credit for safety in times of tragedy, and in provision of the spiritual benefit.
Example Instruments of love	– ditto	Forgiveness of sins committed previously (Rom. 3:25). It saved all from alienation from God. Love is the keystone of grace. It was by this grace we were all saved (Eph. 2:8).
Instruments of Rightesousness	– ditto	Provides a platform for the working of faith. Enables one to produce fruit of the Spirit (Gal. 5:22-23), and have divine virtues (Mt. 5:3-12)
Instument of Spirit of faith	– ditto	Prompts man to have faith, which is akin to surrender to God (Dan. 3:23-26)

The Table of Favour

Heaven	Kingdom of God confined within man (inert light)	Life on earth
Wisdom from God	*Imprint of reign in times of ignorance, and now (Acts 17:30).*	*Favour (Compassion for life – Ps. 30:5b)*
	Expression of mercy of God	Fulfilmet of the promise of a blessing of earthly form: greatness, possession of stuff, child, fame, generosity, help, power and prosperity of tangibles (Gen. 12:2, 3a)
Example Instrument of kindness	Ditto	Blessing earthly things: money and stock
Instuments of compassion	Ditto	The law, that man may know sin and reveal his inadequacy in the plan of God (Gal. 3:19)
Instrument of capability	Ditto	Power to make wealth (Deut. 8:18)
Insturment of mercy	Ditto	Safety from bodily harm (Acts 14:19-20).
Instrument of wisdom	Ditto	Acts wisely, wise judgement, knowledge, understanding and so on (Deut. 1:8).

Lesson from the tables of grace and favour

- *Favour* yields the benefit of *earthly nature*.
- G*race* yields ingredient of *heavenly nature*.
- *Both grace and favour are unmerited, or undeserved.*

But they mean different things. Any instruments of governance in heavenly government may produce the imprint of either favour to meet the promise of earthly things by God, or grace to meet divine requirement for man to please God.

In comparison, the heavenly instrument of governance is similar to the instrument of governance in human governance (army, police and so on).

The authority which the instrument of governance exerts in human governance is like the imprint in the case of heavenly governance.

The benefit to man in either case is neither the authority, nor the imprint. Rather, it is the result of either of them that matters to man. That is, either space to live in freedom or grace respectively.

The keystone by love gave rise to the common salvation for all men (Jude 3a). Besides the common salvation, God does not desire that anybody should perish. So He further made grace to be available to every man to access through faith for his benefit daily (Jude 3b). This is the grace obtained by faith.

Now that man has been forgiven the previous sins, all that he has to do to profit from it is to believe in Jesus. It is only then that God will revive His kingdom in his heart. This is represented by the plane of stars in the illustration above.

Below the plane of stars is the kingdom of darkness into which every man is born and manipulated by the spirit of error (Rom. 7:15, 17 and 23).

In dreams man operates between the contending realms of spirit within him in line with the working of his mind and spiritual inclination (Lk. 17:20–21). But at mortal death, man is pulled back to the main domain of the spirit realm, which he might have chosen by his faith and works, or lack of them (Eccl. 12:7; Lk. 16:19–31).

The reign of Christ reveals itself in the life of man from time to time by the imprint of the appropriate instrument of governance. This is how Christ shows His presence in the life of man to find grace to live a Christlike life.

(A detailed deliberation on grace and truth is available in the 2014 title *The Choice is Yours*, which is accessible for free online reading at www.christthelordreign.com.)

The difference between grace and favour

The grace of God flows solely from above to man for His sake (Is. 43:25). When grace is upon man, the glory of God, which no man has right to share with Him, is manifested for men to notice and to then give praise to Him (1 Pet. 3:14). The caveat is that man has to first believe in Jesus and have faith to get the benefit of the grace of God.

On the other hand, favour is a gift from above and there is no precondition attached (Lk. 1:28–30). Unlike grace, favour from God can be to both the believer and unbeliever, and the substance is basically mammon in form. In which case, favour might be misused to pervert the affairs of God, as happened in the episode of King Saul and of those who perished in the wilderness.

Grace addresses the fulfilment of the promise of heavenly nature (Is. 41:27; Gal. 3:8)

On the other hand, favour addresses the fulfilment of the blessings of a worldly nature (Gal. 3:14).

It was by grace that the blood of Jesus was shed to save man. This is what made the way for man to return home to God in heaven at His appointed time (Col. 1:12–14).

But favour resulted in the shedding of the blood of animals to appease God, that He might cover the sins of man.

The two levels of grace (Jude 3)

These are the grace of resurrection or common salvation, and the grace received by faith to work out one's own salvation.

A. The grace of resurrection or common salvation

This grace was given free to all without input by man. God gave it to fulfil the promise He made to Himself and to Abraham (Gen. 3:15, 12:3b; Titus 1:2).

It is this grace which saved all from the sins committed in the past, and from all previous curses (Rom. 3:25–26; Acts 14:16).

The specific deliverables of grace of common salvation

1. The annulment of the divide erected by sin and the law in ordinances which had alienated man from God (Eph. 2:14–15).2
2. Provision of the Way by the blood of Jesus to the Kingdom of God.
3. Removal of the divide which was erected by the law of ordinance and covenant which separated the Jews and Gentiles. This made one man from the two (Eph. 2:14–15).
4. Invite of all men in darkness to the light of God.
5. Reconciliation of the one man to God, thus making peace, that man might be the righteousness of God by faith in Christ (Mt. 27:51).
6. Unhindered access to God for all till the day of Judgment.

Until the day of the Lord the unhindered access to the Kingdom of God will remain in place for all to accept the free gift of salvation of common grace.

It is then that everyone shall be judged on account of his faith and works in the body of Christ (2 Cor. 5:10).

The common salvation by grace was solely for the sake of redeeming God's name, and therefore it was not a favour done to man (Ps. 23:3).

This suggests that whoever has accepted to profit from it is to hold on to the benevolence by abiding in Christ always (Rom. 8:1; Acts 17:30) – *obey His commandments and walk like Him* (1 John 2:5–6). If, however, a man who has believed backslides, he is to confess and repent, that the blood of Jesus might cleanse him immediately and be restored (1 John 1: 7, 9). The man who denies confession and repentance will be condemned (Ezek. 18: 24). Any contrary understanding of forgiveness by grace certainly suggests a defect in the reading of the scripture (Jude 4).

Illustration of the grace of resurrection

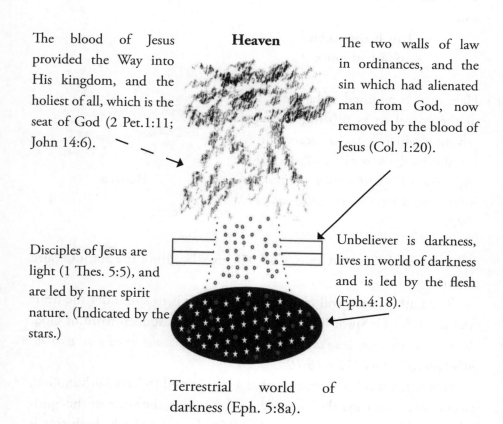

The blood of Jesus provided the Way into His kingdom, and the holiest of all, which is the seat of God (2 Pet.1:11; John 14:6).

Heaven

The two walls of law in ordinances, and the sin which had alienated man from God, now removed by the blood of Jesus (Col. 1:20).

Disciples of Jesus are light (1 Thes. 5:5), and are led by inner spirit nature. (Indicated by the stars.)

Unbeliever is darkness, lives in world of darkness and is led by the flesh (Eph.4:18).

Terrestrial world of darkness (Eph. 5:8a).

B. The grace received by faith for daily living

The grace received by faith is to demonstrate the just righteousness of God.

**This is the second
phase of grace.**

Here man is required to have the faith of the gospel so as to profit from the salvation which Jesus has accomplished for him by the first phase of grace (Jude 3b). *This is the faith which is required by man to work out his own salvation (Phil. 2:12).*

Heaven

When a man believes in Jesus, God will give the gift of the Spirit of faith to him.

The faith of man will be his response. This is to surrender the heart and mind to the Spirit by obeying the written or spoken word of God. *In practice, the man is to say and do only that which the word says, without other consideration (John 15:10).*

It is when this is the practice that a man is said to have faith in God. In essence, it portrays the surrender of the man to the voice of the Spirit of God. This practice eliminates self-effort. In other words, faith stands man in the grace of God, making it the means to succumb to the reign of Christ.

In which case, the man will watch as the instruments of governance do as he desires, making him shine with the strength of Christ (Mt. 5:16; Phil. 4:13). Then he will begin to reign in life by faith through the working of the instruments of governance of the reign of Christ in his favour (Rom. 5:17).

This is an example of how to identify oneself as a spirit-man, and to walk in the Spirit on earth (2 Cor.5:16), knowing that the word of God is Spirit (John 6:63).

The behaviour will be akin to those who produce the fruit of the Spirit (Gal. 5:22–23).

This is the daily saving grace of precious common faith which God gave to everybody who believed (2 Pet. 1:1). That the faith is common to all who chose to believe in Jesus makes the righteousness of God just (Acts 17:30).

In working out one's own salvation, emulate the conduct of Apostle Paul in handling the gospel of Christ in the open and in private life (Phil. 1:27). Focus on the ministration of the word of God, and not on earthly things (Acts 6:4). Daily, give praise, thanksgiving and prayers to God.

How to grow in grace

The suggested proven definition of the grace of God from the viewpoint of the Holy Bible is that it is the imprint of the reign of the Lord Jesus Christ.

This diagnosis is as described previously.

More knowledge on grace is available in the 2014 title *The Choice is Yours*, which is free to read online at www.christthelordreign.com.

The love of God produced the imprint within the heart of man, or grace to use the earthly label. This grace saved all from the sins committed up to the moment a man decides to believe in Jesus (Rom. 3:25). From that moment onward, the grace upon man trickles in proportion with his faith. This suggests that the extent to which you put God first, in dealings will boost how often you have faith that stands you in grace.

Once you stand in grace the reign of Christ will do all the things you desire, through you as a vessel. Those who observe you will think you are the doer.

This suggests that to have faith is to surrender self-effort to God and let Him do all things through you (Phil. 4:13). So the more a man increases his study of the scriptures and meditates on it and obeys, the more Christ will reign in his life.

This is the way to grow in grace or experience more of the grace of God.

Thus to grow in grace is not by increase in possession of earthly things, which is due to favour (Acts 14:17).

Chapter Twenty-One

Righteousness: the Mystery of Investiture

The scriptures have from inception declared three stages of investiture of righteousness of God in Christ for man to completely be righteous like Christ it suggests why man is being justified freely by Grace (Rm. 3:24). However people have been misled to believe that once a man 'claims' to believe in Jesus he has become born again. What is not obvious to many is that to 'believe' in Jesus involves a total change to the lifestyle of Jesus. This is who is a disciple of Jesus.

'The meaning of believe can be read free at www.christtheloedreign. com in the 2013 title of Return to God'.

Generally there are the righteousness of man, that of the law, and of God in Christ.

The righteousness of God in Christ is our focus here.

According to the scriptures, the kingdom of God is righteousness and peace and joy in the Holy Spirit (Rom. 14:17). In the same vein, it was prophesied that the Saviour is Jesus Christ the Lord, our righteousness (Jer. 23:6).

An examination of the two statements will show that righteousness is not linked with the actions of man (Lk. 18:11–12, 14).

This suggests that it is a misreading of the scriptures to believe that righteousness is to live right with God, or believe right. Instead, righteousness is the sacred needs of man and they are divine attributes in Christ.

As a result, the *righteousness of God in Christ is a gift of godly privileges to man* through the combination of grace and faith (Rom. 5:17).

Therefore, the righteousness which is to the credit of man is the manifestation of the character of God in his life – manners, relationships, love, joy, humbleness, fruit of righteousness, fruit of the Spirit, and so on (Lk. 18:13–14).

In the salvation scheme of God He programmed the spirit, soul and body (1 Thes. 5:23) to receive the gift of righteousness as an award at different times.

This suggests the reason why Jesus finished the work of salvation, but cut it short of righteousness. It is to keep man on his toes to fear God, that he might be watchful not to suffer the fate of Sodom and Gomorrah (Rom. 9:28).

So from the onset of the new creation, the new spirit alone was made and adorned with the investiture of complete righteousness and holiness (Eph. 4:24). So when a man believes in Jesus like Adam believed in God, this gift of righteousness is given to him (Rom. 4:3, 5).

At the same time, both the soul and body are awarded righteousness and holiness, but they have to wait patiently to be adorned with the investiture. This is how Jesus cut short His finished work in righteousness, as stated previously. It is the reason why all believers can now only believe and know and do and see things in part (1 Cor. 13:12).

Now Jesus has made ready the complete righteousness for spirit, soul and body. When a man (truly) believes, the spirit which God gives to him is straightaway adorned with righteousness and holiness. As the man runs the race of life according to the will of God, his soul will gradually be transformed to the image of Christ by the Holy Spirit (2 Cor. 3:18). Then the soul will be prepared to be adorned with the investiture of righteousness and holiness at an appointed time.

On the basis of the already awarded righteousness to man as a whole, he might increase and abound in the love of all. Doing this might make God to establish his heart blameless in holiness (1 Thes. 3:13). Any man who has been given the new creation Spirit can say that he is righteous while he patiently waits in hope for the investiture of his soul and body. It is by the last day that the body will receive the benefit of investiture of righteousness (Rom. 8:11). Then the man as a whole shall receive the crown of righteousness as a prize for successfully completing the race of life, and becomes blameless and holy before God (2 Tim. 4:8).

The crown of righteousness which will make man a partaker in the reign of Christ, with the rights to deploy the instrument of governance, is the evidence of things not seen in the Holy Bible's description of faith (Heb. 11:1). It explains why salvation of the soul will be the end of faith (1 Pet. 1:9).

Tracing the way of righteousness of earthly life

Adam was created upright (Eccl. 7:29)

In the beginning God made Adam righteous in His image and likeness (Gen. 1:27).

But because he ate the fruit of the knowledge of good and evil, he opted out of the godly privileges of righteousness.

As a result of his disobedience he has to die in accordance with the rule set by God (Gen. 2:17). So every descendant of Adam died as a sinner and a slave to sin in his loins (John 8:34). To this day this has remained the reason for man to commit sin, and not that his committing sin makes him a sinner. Therefore nobody is righteous or can do what will make him righteous or good (Eccl. 7:20).

This means nobody could save himself or another from the sin committed (Ps. 49:6–7). The experience of Adam clearly suggests that the man who has been saved once can lose his salvation if he disobeys God at any time afterwards and fails to confess and repent (Ezek. 18:24).

In one man, Adam, all died

The first Adam had the entire mankind in his loins when he committed sin. As a result all men sinned together.

Therefore when Adam disobeyed and died, mankind also disobeyed God and died. By this death every man became blind and deaf and dull in heart (Isa. 35:5; 42: 7, 16). As a result, every man is born on earth in this state (Ps. 51:5).

However, this blanket effect is not the same in salvation of the soul by

Jesus, the second Adam. As a result, not all will be raised alive like Christ. This is the caveat in the scripture (1 Cor. 15:22–23). It is no longer a group salvation of the soul, unlike in the case of Adam. Rather, it will be of a personal choice. Abraham was the first man to receive the promise of the design of God to save man (Gen, 12:3c).

Abraham was the father of righteousness of faith (Rom. 4:11)
Abraham

God found Abram and made him the link between the dead and eternal life. So God made promises of earthly and heavenly nature to Abram (Gen. 12.1–3).

The earthly pertain to name, material needs and human issues. God later changed Abram's name to Abraham, and he was indeed blessed with earthly things. To fulfill the promise of the heavenly nature, God promised Abraham the son of promise, who was born as Isaac. In his loins was the hope of the promise of resurrection, which is the heavenly nature (Acts 26:6).

Abraham passed the test of faith. So God established faith as the link between the living dead and eternal life in him and in Christ (John 17:3).

Abraham believed in God, and He adjudged it to him for righteousness (Gen. 15:6).

This suggests that to believe in God opens the window of heaven for man to receive divine gifts like righteousness, the spirit of faith (2 Cor. 4:13), and so on.

However, Abraham did not receive the substance of righteousness, which is the investiture. But he saw them from far off and remained in faith to the end, waiting patiently in hope (Heb. 11:39).

Later God gave the law to the descendants of Abraham. It passed through the lineage of Israel and it was adjudged the righteousness of the law, but it did not benefit them. The child of promise joined through the loins of some selected descendants of Abraham, who lived by the righteousness of the law. Finally the seed of Abraham, who was the child of promise, was born as the Son of God (Gen. 12:3c).

Righteousness of God in Christ

The righteousness of the descendants of Abraham was not profitable. Therefore a new righteousness arose which was premised on the covenant by the blood of Jesus. As a result, Jesus was sacrificed on the cross and He became the mercy seat through His blood, by faith. This was to demonstrate the righteousness of God that He might forgive man the sins committed in the past. This was aimed at the reconciliation of man with God, even though he was then a sinner and fell short of His glory (Rom. 5:8).

In the final analysis the sacrifice formed the justification for God to forgive man the sins which were committed previously (Rom. 3:25). The foregoing formed the root of the abundance of grace and the gift of righteousness of God in Christ (Rom. 5:17).

Now that the gift is given without discrimination to all who chose to (truly) believe in Jesus, it demonstrates the just righteousness of God.

Although Jesus finished the work of salvation of man in His first coming, He made it short by staggering the time for the spirit, soul and boy to receive the robe of righteousness and holiness, as previously seen (Rom. 9:28).

Jesus is the Lamb who, before the foundation of the world, volunteered to serve man. So He suffered and was crucified as the sins of man. As a result, God forgave man the sins he committed in the past (Rom. 3:25). This saved all instantly to stand on equal point before God by choice of individual (Deut.30:19).

Second Adam (Jesus)

This left man with the choice to either believes and be given the award of righteousness, or not to believe (Deut. 39:19). The consequence of refusal to believe is to die in the likeness of Adam in Eden (Deut. 30:19).

The righteousness at stake here is of God in Christ Jesus (2 Cor. 5:21).

All that is required is to believe in Jesus. Then God will count the belief to the man for righteousness, as was done to Abraham (Rom. 4:5). Then he will have to wait patiently with hope to be adorned in spirit, soul and body at the appointed time, with the investiture of the already awarded righteousness. The first investiture is on the new Spirit created in righteousness and holiness to dwell in the heart of the man (Eph. 4:24). Then the gradual transformation of the soul will follow, as seen previously.

When a sinner turns away from sin to embrace the righteousness of God in Christ, he shall be forgiven the sins he committed previously (Ezek. 18:21–22).

There is no middle space between righteousness and unrighteousness because man cannot faithfully serve God and Mammon (Mt. 6:24).

What is true is that no man shall be judged again regarding the sins for which Jesus died on the cross. But every man shall be judged for his subsequent works in the body of Christ (2 Cor. 5:10).

The differences between 'all died in Adam' and 'that all might live in Christ' (1 Cor. 15:22)

All that died in one man, Adam, were in his loins when it happened. But all that might be saved by one man, Jesus Christ, were not in His loins, but rather in darkness. *As a result, every man has to first confess with his mouth the Lord Jesus, and believe in his heart that God has raised Him from the dead. It is then God will give to him the badge of common salvation by grace (Rom. 10:9).* This is the qualification for man to take position on the starting line of the race of life to work out his own salvation for an incorruptible prize: the crown of righteousness and the reward for the work he did in the body of Christ.

The Race of Life

Starting line of the race for all to work out their own salvation (Phil. 2:12)

The race by faith

Finishing line (day of judgment)

Prize shall include:
Crown of Righteousness (2 Tim. 4:8), Morning Star (2 Pet. 1:19),
Salvation of Soul (1 Pet. 1:9) and reward of sitting and ruling with
Christ (Rev. 2:26, 3:21-22) or Condemnation.

Remarks

1. Until a man believes in Jesus he will live in darkness behind the starting line. This man will end up in condemnation on the day of judgment (Dan. 12:2b).
2. The sins which a man may commit during the race shall be washed away by the blood of Jesus if he confesses and repents from the sins (1 John 1:9).
3. But a racer who backslides and fails to confess and repent will lose both his righteousness and righteous deeds, and he will die (Ezek. 18:24). (The man who died because Adam died was in his loins; therefore it was the same thing that happened to him and Adam.)

But righteousness in Christ is of God. It is given to whomever desires it. Therefore it may be withdrawn from an unrepentant backslider who once believed and enjoyed the goodness of God (Heb. 6:4–6).

4. a) The promise of hope of resurrection which God made to Abraham is the same as to seek the kingdom of God and His righteousness.
    b) The promise of God to Abraham is same as what the scripture assured man of if he first seeks the kingdom and His righteousness (Mt. 6:33).

Virtue and dislike of righteousness of God in Christ

Virtue of righteousness of God

- Waits patiently in hope to receive the crown of righteousness (2 Tim. 4:8).
- Careful not to disobey God; knows that he has only been forgiven his past sins (Rom. 3:25).
- Hopes to be like Christ (1 John 3:2–3)
- Preaches and accepts only the gospel of grace (1 Cor. 2:2).
- Sets mind on the things above and not the things on earth (Rom. 8:5; Col.3:2–4).
- Produces fruit of Spirit as a lifestyle, etc. (Mic. 6:8; Gal. 5:22–23).

Dislike of righteousness of God

- Flirts with the law (Jer. 3:16).
- Does things of sin (Gal. 5:19–21).
- Returns to old habits and the law (Gal. 2:17–18).
- Perverse doctrine of forgiveness which denies the word of God
- (Ezek. 18: 24; 1 John 3:8–10).
- Doctrine of earthly things like materialism, fables, wonders, etc. 2 Pet. 2:1–3; 1 Tim. 4:1–2; 2 Tim.4:3–4).
- Regulations and commandment of man (establishment and individual).

Experience has shown that man cannot be relied upon (John 2:24). Even God once regretted creating man because of his evil inclinations (Gen. 6:6).

Is the blood of Christ so common, and of no effect to forgive sins yet to be committed? Everybody shall be judged before Christ the Lord (2 Cor. 5:10; Rom. 14:12). This judgment of the believer shall be about the reaping of what he sowed to either flesh or spirit (Gal. 6:7–8).

Evidence of righteousness of God in Christ on earth

On earth there are members of the righteousness of God. The scripture describes them as the fruit of the Spirit (Gal. 5:22–23). It means the fruit is spirit in form.

This is in conjunction with God's wisdom, knowledge and understanding.

The Lord Jesus Christ is the sole maker of the fruit. The man who is joined to Him manifests the fruit daily as proof of his walk in the Spirit (John 15:4–5). *So righteousness is not to believe right or do right, but to be a holy characteristic of God.*

Fruitless branch (unbeliever)

Produces nothing because he is not joined to Christ, the vine (John 15:6).

Unbeliever remains as darkness (Eph. 4:18).

Branch (Paul)

Produces fruit of the spirit as a daily lifestyle: (Gal. 5:22–23; James 1:27; 3:13–16; Titus 3:1–3; Mt. 25:34–36; Is. 1:17 etc.)

Branch (disciple)

Produces fruit of the Spirit as a daily lifestyle (Gal. 5:22–23; James 1:27; 3:13–16; Mt. 25:34–36; Is. 1:17; Titus 3:1–3 etc.)

Vine (Lord)

Chapter Twenty-Two

Now Saved, Man is Free From Previous Curses

The setting

The predicament of man dated back to the moment Adam disobeyed the authority of God in the Garden of Eden. He disobeyed the first law of God, which forbade him to eat the fruit of the tree of the knowledge of good and evil. So he has to die in fulfilment of the word of God (Gen. 2:16–17).

In addition, God cursed him and then drove him out of Eden. Also, God cursed the ground from which man was formed in the beginning (Gen. 3:17).

Adam became darkness due to his forgetfulness of the ways of God (Eph. 5:8a). He later compounded his woes by changing the glory of God into an image made like corruptible man, and other mammals and reptiles and physical features of creation (Rom. 1:23). *This was the beginning of idol worship by man.*

Therefore, God further cursed man by giving him up to the lust of his heart to dishonour his body, take lie for truth, worship and serve the creatures instead of Him, and to do other abominations (Rom. 1:24–32).

In his blindness and dull heart, man actually made idols for himself, and built shrines. Then he began to worship and to serve them as though they were the medium to reach and hear from the true God (Is. 6:9–10).

So man made vows to the shrines, and some were unfulfilled. This attracted further curses to man and his descendants. As a result of the wickedness of man, men directed curses at one another from time to time, and eventually this caught up with many and their descendants.

Even those who received the law of Moses did not find reprieve. Instead God lined up a gamut of curses upon failure to obey the laws in full (Deut. 28:15–68).

The mind was further blinded when man could not look at the glowing face of Moses when he first came down with the Ten Commandments from the mountain where he encountered God (2 Cor. 3:14). While this lasted, God turned His back on the Gentiles and allowed them to multiply and wallow in their abominations.

On the other hand, Israel and Judah rebelled against the law of God by building temples for idols. Inside the secret shrines man worshipped and made sacrifice to foreign gods, and so incurred the wrath of God (Hos. 8:14).

Abominations in the temples soared, and all manners of evil were committed in secret places within (Ezek. 8:8–11). Secret covenants of varying degrees were made and entered into by members, with the accompanying curses for failure to abide in them. Members tied their descendants to these abominations and the curses which accompanied them. Individuals sought quick-fix solutions in cults, and as part of the requirements, swore to the shrines and thus embraced the accompanying curses. All these and more evil traditions and practices constituted the curses which have been hunting man to this day.

The acquittal

The reprieve from all the curses came by way of salvation through God Himself. This was based on own counsel without any input from someone else.

At first God wiped a large number of His creations from the face of the earh with a flood of water because of their abominations. But he saved a remnant of the household of Noah from mortal death by means of the ark of Noah, which He earlier commanded him to build (Gen. 8:18–19). This was a time of blindness and ignorance of man, and so God did not reckon any misdeed against him (Lk. 6:39; Acts 17:30a; Rom. 5:13).

Secondly, God later chose to accommodate Israel alone amongst all the nations on earth, and thus dissuade them from living in self-righteousness. This was the first unmerited and undeserved favour to Israel. For this purpose He gave the law to Israel through Moses. This was to stir them to do away with evil works, and make them to know sin. It was also to prepare their minds to learn to worship Him by the faith which was to come (Ex. 31:18).

But the law was not profitable to Israel because she was unable to obey it for the intended effect (Acts 15:10). Rather, the law became the strength of sin. How?

The favour through the law made man to know what sin is. It stirred all kinds of evil desires which drove man to explore what the law was shielding.

As a result, the law caused man to fall into further transgressions and commit additional sins (Rom. 3:20).

By hiding under the requirements of the law, men of higher standing in the establishment took advantage of it to put the heavy burden of yoke upon others of lesser standing for their personal benefits. In addition, Israel, after the flesh, slipped back to the worship of idols from time to time (1 King 11:4).

Thirdly and finally, reprieve came when Jesus was born as our Saviour (Lk. 2:11). God had given Him the mandate to give sight to the blind, open the ears of the deaf and restore life to man (Lk. 4:18; Is. 35:5; Mt. 9:27–31). At the end of His ministry He was crucified and buried, but three days later He came back from the dead; the first to have ever done so (Rom. 6:3–5).

The shed blood of Jesus became the justification of man for God to forgive him the sins that were committed in the past, making Him the just and the justifier of the man who has faith in His Son (Rom. 3:25–26). This finished work of Jesus sanctified all and made all men holy before God (Heb. 10:10). *It wiped out completely every sin, iniquity, transgression and curse that existed against man in the past (Gal. 3:13–14; Col. 2:13–14).*

The choice to accept or reject Jesus now rests on each man

The believer is a new creation and his choice will be to imitate Jesus and so be His disciple, which is different from just being a Christian (1 Cor. 11:1). But he is to realise that it is the spirit alone that has been renewed (Eph. 4:24).

The soul and body shall be fully transformed to manifest their form of the new creation at the time God appointed for each (2 Cor. 3:18; Rom. 8:11).

This requires man to hold fast to the finished works of Jesus, forgetting the past; then work out his own salvation by adhering to the gospel of Jesus crucified. Obey the commandments of the love of God, and carry your cross daily.

Putting God first
(The key to an excellent life, and to increase in faith in God)

The evidence that a man has been saved is that he puts God first, and can be seen to do so in all things. It is first to realise that God is in the likeness of a potter and that man is in the likeness of clay to Him. So the first way to put God first is to yield only to Him, that He might be pleased to mould the individual into a good vessel. To yield to God implies single-mindedness towards Him.

This is the key to excellence, and the principle of faith in the Lord (Prov. 4:20).

In the process Christ is allowed to increase, and you decrease, in every decision made, and in the execution process (John 3:30). This is the only way to keep to the oath of creation, which is that man is the image and likeness of God. So do nothing that might make you unworthy of Him. To do this is to obey God's commandments, increase and abound in love to all, and walk like Jesus (1 John 2:3, 6).

Notice that to put God first is engineered in the heart. The visible execution is a manifestation of what has been done in the spirit realm

(Prov. 3:6; Eph. 6:5–7). Do all things concerning eternity by faith in God.

To be single-minded towards God is not without challenges. There will be name-calling, hatred, persecution and the like, which have to be endured as the cross that is carried daily (Mt. 16:24).

The high side of putting God first is that it is the key to excellent living, and to increasing and abounding in faith in God.

Key to excellence

When you put God first He becomes your motivation in what you say and do. As a result you will begin to regard your work at all times as a labour to please the Lord (Gal. 3:23). In which case, every other thing (remuneration, profit, pain, persecution and so on) becomes secondary and something that you can live with. By this behaviour you will be like a light amongst men – family members, co-workers, business competitors and partners, and local church members (Mt. 5:1415). This will stand you out as a model amongst men, and therefore becomes an epistle of the gospel of Jesus crucified to them (2 Cor. 3:2–3).

An excellence in labour alone might become, to some, an unsolicited but irresistible attraction, which may make those who observe the good work of the man give glory to God, and possibly believe in Christ (Dan. 6:25–27; Acts 8:12–13).

Then the way of life of the man will be a normal behaviour which daily produces the fruit of the Spirit such as love, joy, self-control and so on (Gal. 5:22–23). This is an attribute that lives on, and which might be remembered on the day of visitation, when men will because of it give glory to God (1 Pet. 2:12).

For anyone who puts God first, the grace of God which saved all will always be available to help in every situation of need (Heb. 4:16).

Increase in faith as a result of putting God first

This is discussed in Chapter 25, and also in Chapter 23 on how to work out your own salvation.

The consequences of denying Jesus

Now God has acquitted man through the propitiation by the blood of Jesus, through faith. Therefore the onus is on him to acknowledge His righteous judgment (Rom. 3:25–26). All that God expects from man is to abide in Christ. It is the only way by which he might bear fruit to please Him (John 15:1–2).

On the day of judgment man might not have the justification of failure to abide in Jesus. This suggests that the man who denied Jesus now chose not to utilise the opportunity of the favour of God by grace to abide in Christ. The risks will be the denial of entry into the kingdom of God. That will be catastrophic for those who will see the saved ones inside while they are locked out (Mt. 13:42).

Crowd of people who denied Jesus wanting to enter the kingdom, but who are shut out and crying and wailing outside the entrance

Patriarchs and saved souls inside

Entrance locked

Kingdom of God

Once the Lord shuts the now-open door, standing outside and knocking will amount to nothing. He will equally deny those who denied Jesus and worked in iniquity. Their weeping and gnashing of the teeth will be in vain (Lk. 13:28).

Chapter Twenty-Three

Faith and Works are Like Siamese Twins

(Read about faith for free online at www.christthelordreign.com *in Article 4 of the title The Choice is Yours.)*

The two kinds of faith

Without faith, man cannot please God (Heb. 11:6). Faith will come to an end after the salvation of the soul (1 Pet. 1:9). *This makes faith a stopgap necessity.*

This suggests that faith is the only antenna by which man can improve his life of darkness in his dwelling realm of darkness. It is the only means to link with God, who dwells in the realm of light in the utmost heaven above (Eccl. 5:2).

But faith has to first cast off its dark nature, and adopt the nature of light. It is for this purpose that the blood of Jesus was shed. It has provided the solution for the faith nature to change to the light nature just through believing in Jesus.

This makes it imperative to really understand what faith means in practical terms. God willing, the opportunity is now here. In general terms, faith alone is incomplete without executing the directive that comes with it, which is the works.

Faith is composed of a voice with an intrinsic directive, which requires to be obeyed. It is the obedience of the intrinsic directive that the scripture refers to as works, and which some now called action. This is why the scripture emphasised that faith without works is dead or incomplete (James 2:22).

As the scripture has declared, faith comes from hearing and hearing (repeatedly) the word of God (Rom. 10:17). *However, care must be taken not to confuse faith in God with faith in the wisdom of man.* Both come by hearing, but the former comes from hearing the word of God while the latter comes from hearing the word of mankind or an extraneous voice of error.

This latter faith is of the carnal mind, or mental faculty. It is by the carnal faith that man obeys the regulations and commandments of men in their local church (Col. 2:20–23). It is the kind of faith which a convert (the lesser being, like a layman) might have in the principal (the higher being, like a pastor), leading him to rely on him for guidance.

So when he hears the principal speak, he will believe without doubt that what he says will surely be. "Switch on the TV," he says, "and you will be amazed by the pastor." Then he switches on the television and indeed he is amazed.

But he, the convert, remains who he has always been in conduct, even though he may receive an additional awareness. This kind of worldly faith is different from faith in God, or in Christ Jesus.

Two major differences separate the two kinds of faith. Namely:
1. The way of hearing and believing
2. The resulting effect on the hearer

Faith of the world's wisdom
1. The faith of the world comes from hearing and believing with mental faculty.
2. It does not lead to any change in the normal behaviour of either the hearer (convert) or the principal (preacher).

Let us examine the example of a principal who has faith in his servant.

By the faith that the principal has in his servant, he gives his command and then expects the servant to obey. But the faith will not change the behaviour or disposition of the principal, and it will not bring credit to the servant either. This is because the servant would have merely done what he was hired to do and it will not cause any change in his usual work schedule and in his behaviour (Lk. 17:7–9).

In this way, the principal had faith in his servant and all things went well normally. But this is not the kind of faith in discipleship.

Faith in God and in Jesus Christ

1. In the faith of man in God, he hears His word and believes it with the heart (Rom. 10:10).
2. The man then abandons his former beliefs and assumes the character and conduct of what he has just heard from God, and believed or accepted.

As a result, man will immediately begin to obey the voice without any choice.

Then he begins to do exactly what he hears and believes as something coming from the lord Jesus Christ, who is the Word of God (John 5: 19, 30).

This obedience of the inherent directive in the voice is what is regarded as the works of Siamese twins, where faith is the hearing partner, or twin.

So if the voice says that it is better to eat fish than to eat chicken, the hearer will immediately stop eating chicken, which he has been accustomed to previously, and will switch the appetite totally to fish. This is the transition of the hitherto unknown or hidden truth by faith into real life. The man who lives by this faith says and does things from the viewpoint of Christ Jesus. This suggests that to have faith in God is to surrender to Him by saying or doing what you hear Him say or see Him do as depicted by His word (John 5:19).

This is the justification of man to stand in grace and become a vessel through which the governance of the reign of Christ does or says all things. But to observers, the man will appear to be the doer. So when the man utters a command the instrument of the Spirit of faith in the reign of Christ actualises it as though the man is the doer (Mk. 11:23–24).

It is in this way that the reign of the Lord manifests Christ to man (John 14; 21).

As a result, the man (hearer) will become a co-heir with Christ Jesus. This will make him a partaker in the deployment of the instrument of His reign, to do humanly impossible things, to the amazement of the uninformed.

(Refer to Chapter 20 on grace to understand how things are done by the instrument of the reign of Christ Jesus).

Let us examine 'faith in God' in practical terms

The scripture expresses this faith as:

Now faith is the substance of things hoped for, the evidence of things not seen (Heb. 11:1).

This faith of God is a gift from the Holy Spirit to man (1 Cor. 13:2). It is known as the spirit of faith, which is of the same value to everyone (2 Pet. 1:1).

Now that faith in God is a gift from Him, the task is that of man to choose to accept his voice, or decline. The voice may come by way of a hunch, a directive in the heart or by personal desire, which may have been triggered by intuition or a benefactor (Mt. 17:20). *The practical way to accept the gift of the spirit is to drink it.*

To drink it is synonymous with making yourself succumb to that voice which you have heard and have accepted to be under the influence of. Another way of saying this is to surrender to the voice as previously discussed, and this is further illustrated as follows: If you have faith in Jesus, you listen and surrender to His voice by Spirit of faith.

Spirit of faith
Beckoning to the man within his heart *(an instrument of the reign of Christ)*

The man
Unaware of the plea of the Spirit of faith to him to listen, believe and have faith in God

A man may hear and believe and obey the voice of the Spirit of faith; then expect that the outcome will ultimately show up. On the other hand, a man may desire something and then wait patiently in hope that the Spirit will do that which he desired in his heart, believing that He is able to do it (Lk. 17: 6, 12–19). It requires man to make himself a willing vessel by doing nothing but rely on Him. It is by the Spirit that all things are done.

In other words, it is Him in whom you have faith that does the work while you are a mere vessel of deployment.

The learning point here is that faith in God takes man away from himself. It makes man instead see self as a co-character in the word of God (Phil. 3:8). In this way every self-effort and every contrary voice to that of the word of God is ignored, no matter the circumstances to self (Dan. 3:16–18).

So man is drawn into the realm of Christ. *This is the practice of surrendering to the word of God and beginning to imitate Christ, or live a Christ-like life (Acts 11:26).*

So with the Christ-like life, the man becomes a co-heir with Christ. This will be his qualification to begin to reign together with Him.

The proof of man's reign with Christ will be an observable change in character and conduct. As a result he will be seen to walk by faith, which will manifest in his capacity to do genuine miracles and healing, and to live a daily life of the fruit of the Spirit (Mk. 11:22–24; Col. 1:12).

The Holy Bible account of 'faith' suggests it is to surrender to God in hope of succumbing to the grace through Christ (1 Pet. 1:13)

Proof

Bible Account	Faith as 'Surrender'.
• Now 'faith' is substance of things hoped for.	• Now 'surrender to reign of Christ' is substance of things hoped for
• 'Evidence of things' not seen	• 'co-heir with Christ' not seen

Substance of things is (the body) of Christ, anything else is shadow (Col. 2:16-17).

So to surrender to the reign of Christ is to become a child of God and therefore Christ-like and co-heir with Him (Rom. 8:17).

This suggests that the Holy Bible's definition of faith may actually be rewritten as *Now faith is the "Christ-like life" hoped for, the "joint reign with Christ" not seen.*

This agrees with the scripture, which declares that man can do all things through Christ who strengthens him (Phil. 4:13).

The scripture additionally put the foregoing in true perspective when it declared that *The Lord has begotten man again to a living hope* (1 Pet. 1:3) and that *salvation of our souls is the end of our faith* (1 Pet. 1:9).

The soul that will be redeemed will be like Christ, and both will live together forever (John 14:3). So there will be no more need for the soul to have faith. This salvation is the end time redemption of the whole body, spirit and soul.

All the three will then be in cohesion in full holiness and righteousness in the form of Christ Jesus, and be a co-heir with Him (1 Pet. 1:5, 8).

How to have faith

To have faith in God starts with believing in the Lord, and that God is what He says He is. This belief is peculiar and different from the common beliefs known to man.

In practical terms, to believe in God is to totally surrender oneself to God by forgoing all old habits and taking up the habits of Jesus, namely sourcing of wisdom and knowledge, kind of associations and so on.

Abandon the old ways of living. Begin to say and do and behave in a similar manner to that in which He spoke and did things and conducted Himself, including type of His food which is to do the will of God (John 4:32).

This is what it means to believe in God: a change of attitude in personality to resemble that of Jesus.

Then be still and wait patiently to hear from God (Ps. 46:10).

Hearing comes through the study of His word and meditation on it (Joshua 1:8), from Him in dreams and visions (Job 33:15–16; 36:9–10) and by listening to the gospel of Jesus crucified (Rom. 10:17).

Soon God will by His own counsel remember His promise to Himself and to Abraham to show compassion to man (Ps. 40:1–3).

It is this obedience that justified God to give the gift of righteousness to man, and first to Abraham (Rom. 4:5). Then immediately it is followed by another gift of the spirit of faith. It is this gift of faith that opens up to man to cultivate his own habit of faith in God through hearing of the voice of the word written for our learning (John 6:63).

The faith will then become the justification for man to stand in the grace of God through Christ (Rom. 5:2). Then man will become a partaker of the inheritance of the saints in light (Col. 1:12). The Holy Spirit will gradually transform the once-frozen DNA of the image and likeness of God in man to the DNA of Christ (3 Cor. 3:18).

As a result the man will always in his behaviour imitate Apostle Paul (1 Cor. 11:1), who also imitated Jesus (2 Cor. 4:13). Then as he believes with the heart, so he will speak. The evidence will be in his walking in Spirit by producing the fruit of the Spirit as a daily behaviour (Gal. 5:22–23).

Faith and works are inseparable twins

Every voice has an inbuilt command. It is to do the intrinsic requirement in the voice of the spirit of faith that is regarded as the works of faith (James 2:17–18). This was how Abraham obeyed God and set out to the promised land, and later also embarked on the journey to sacrifice Isaac, his only son (Gen. 22:10).

Therefore the works which accompany faith are different from the works of the righteousness of the law, or self-righteousness or man-designed.

Unlike the works of faith, these later works are purposed in the mind by man to achieve a set target with the intent of gain. This deceitfully makes man boast and give credit to his own effort regarding the gain made (1 Tim.6:9–1).

But as it has been previously examined, the spirit of faith is an instrument of governance of the reign of Christ Jesus. Therefore to have faith is to let the reign of Christ do what is required to be done through you by giving up self-effort.

So in all cases, you rely on Christ and stop thinking of or putting hope in any other source. In this way you succumb to the entreaty of the spirit of faith.

Then the imprint of the apt instrument of governance of the reign of Christ will act on your thoughts and be decoded as grace that produced the desired results. It might be to protect man from harm, or to accord him blessing, or to provide care and health, or move mountain and so on (Mk. 11:23–24; Dan. 3:16–18).

Faith lifts man to stand in the grace and be in the same Spirit realm with God. It is only then that he will really hear the true message of Christ and believe with the heart. Then he will speak as a vessel of the Lord Jesus (2 Cor. 4:13). This is when the man will begin to imitate Jesus Christ, and to do things according to the viewpoint of God. At this stage the man of faith has changed from the lifestyle of self-righteousness to total dependence on God to do anything (John 5:1920).

The man becomes the vessel through whom Christ in him expresses His viewpoint (John 14:21). This is an example of submission to God (James 4:7).

The faith of man stirs the compassion of God to remember His promise to His preordained child in the solid foundation that has been laid, which is Jesus (Heb. 11:6).This stimulates the desire of God to transform the predestined child, by the Holy Spirit, to adoption by Jesus to Him, for His pleasure.

Why the transformation?

Now the body and spirit of man who might believe in Jesus have been killed along with Him. So God created new spirit and body for man in Christ (Eph. 2:10). However his soul which God created in His image and likeness was spared and the soul which He prepared in Jesus for sacrifice was killed in his place (Is. 53:10).

But when Adam began to live by the DNA of own image and likeness the soul-man who previously had the DNA of God got frozen to preserve it (Gen.5:3).

Thus the transformation is to energise the frozen DNA of the 'image and likeness of God' to conform to the image of Christ (2 Cor. 3:18).

It is the faith which justified man who has chosen to abide in Christ against evil done towards him, that he might be glorified in Christ in line with the prayer and desire of Jesus (Rom. 8:29–30). This accomplishment is the testimony of the fulfilment of the promise which God made to restore life to man for the sake of His name (Ps. 23:3).

As it has been examined previously, "faith" and "works" go together as twins, which enables man to abide in Christ and to be able to produce and live as the fruit of the spirit (Gal. 5:22–23).

The growth in faith

God has given to every man the same measure of faith. Thus everybody who truly believed in Jesus received the same Spirit of faith (2 Pet. 1:1).

It is by the strength of this Spirit of faith that each man is prompted to have his own faith, which varies between individuals.

So, there is weak faith, little faith, great faith, and so on (Rom. 14:1; Mt. 8:26; Lk. 7:9). This variation might be due to how often one hears and believes the word of truth or the famine of knowledge and understanding amongst men (Rom. 10:17).

God made man to please Him and he can only do this by first knowing that He is the only true God and the Light. This light is invisible and so man can only walk in it by faith to please God (2 Cor. 5:7; Heb. 11:6).

Then he can walk according to His will which is for man to be the adopted sons by Jesus Christ (Eph. 1:5, 9; Phil. 2:13).

This suggests that man has to first seek the Kingdom of God and His righteousness and put Him first in all his dealings in life (Prov. 3:6, Mt. 6:33).

No man can connect to God without faith. But it is only when man is connected to God that He will give him the grace to receive knowledge and understanding, and to do things which are beyond the strength and wisdom of ordinary man (Mt. 17:20). The capacity to ward off sicknesses (James 5:15), or to defend oneself against adversity (Eph. 6:15), or to walk with God, or to have a true relationship with God, as to please Him is only by faith of any level (Heb. 11: 6).

The closer and more steadfast a man is to God, the more he will step up in faith, which is to surrender to Him because of belief in his inadequacy without Christ (Rom. 1:17). This suggests that to grow in faith is to give up incrementally the old ways of thinking and of doing things by self-effort, and to steadily turn to God, putting Him first in all thinking and actions. It can begin by loving others as God has loved us. Then believe only in the word of God as it is written, and stop looking elsewhere for solutions to your challenges.

Let your motivation in the service you provide to others be the hope for the crown of righteousness.

Chapter Twenty-Four

The Principle of Forgiveness

Master forgave debtor (A) after begging him.

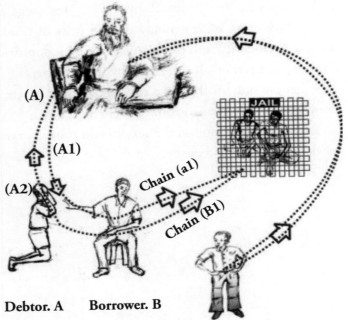

Master Mt. 18:23)

Master changed his mind and sent debtor to prison (A1) until he paid his debt for not forgiving the borrower (B) (Mt. 18:32–34)

(A)

(A1)

(A2)

Chain (a1)

Chain (B1)

(B1)

Debtor. A   Borrower. B

Debtor begged master for forgiveness(A2) (Mt. 18:24–27)

Borrower begged debtor for forgiveness (B), but instead he sent him to jail (Mt. 18:29–30)

Tale-bearer observed debtor and borrower and reported debtor to the master (Mt. 18:31)

Lessons of forgiveness

In the illustration the Lord is in the likeness of the master of the debtor, and the debtor is in the likeness of man (Mt. 23:10).

God made and owns all things in the heavens and on earth. Every man is therefore a debtor to Him with regards to his life and all he possesses (Ps. 24:1).

Right from the moment Adam, and later man, committed abominable sins against God man has been worthy of death (Gen. 3:6; Mal. 2:11). Nonetheless God sacrificed His only begotten Son Jesus, to be His justification to forgive man, through faith, of the sins committed previously. As a result He forgave man the sins that were committed in the past (Rom. 3:25).

Now all that any man has, he has received from God. So he is to show mercy to the fellow man who borrows from him, in a similar manner to that in which God has demonstrated forgiveness to man. A benefactor is to show the same compassion which God has shown to him to his beneficiary. In the event of a benefactor declining to show similar compassion to his beneficiary, God will rescind His earlier forgiveness to the benefactor. As a result, God will demand from him all that he owes Him, and put him in jail to be tormented until he pays all his debt.

In a similar way, God will justifiably rescind His earlier forgiveness of the past sins which the unforgiving man committed (Ezek. 18:24; Rom, 3:25). Like the benefactor has done to the man who borrows from him but refused to heed his entreaty, God will do same to him. He will equally throw the unforgiving servant into the bondage of darkness to be tormented in the same way that he has dealt with the man who borrows from him. The man will be worse off because he can never pay for the sins he has committed.

So every man who expects God to forgive him his sins must first forgive his debtor(s). This puts a demand on every man to imitate Jesus and cultivate the character of forgiveness in every area of life (Col. 3:13).

Effects of a lack of forgiveness

Apart from the rebound effect of a lack of forgiveness as previously highlighted, there is more devastating effect for the unforgiving man.

A lack of forgiveness leads the mind to roam and to unearth the ugly side of man towards the supposed offender.

This may cause internal tension, worries, sleeplessness, distrust, self-inflicted pain, clinical depression and anger, which may lead to revenge. Any of these stressors might lead to internal disorder of organs. The consequences might be possible malfunctioning of body parts, irritation, aggression mood, sleeplessness and poor work output.

Worse still is that the foregoing might cause the aggrieved to develop self-destructive trauma in his inner nature and in his body. This may result in disorientation and loss of self-confidence. Meanwhile the debtor, apart from his incarceration, may be more at peace with himself than the unforgiving benefactor.

Chapter Twenty-Five

The Unrighteous Mammon

The dictionary defines 'mammon' as 'material wealth or possession'. It may therefore sound easy to identify mammon in general. Certainly such reasoning sounds true from the perspective of worldly wisdom. But from the viewpoint of the scriptures the reasoning might be misplaced. In the eyes of God, 'mammon' means much more than the dictionary definition.

The scripture has established that mammon is anything, including man, which can attract the heart away from pleasing God (Gal. 1:10).

Jesus affirmed this when He approved the choice made by Martha to cling to Him and learn of the kingdom of God rather than to be preoccupied with the affairs of the table or stomach, which Mary chose (Lk. 10:41).

This suggests that to first focus on self-preservation in preference to the affairs of God is to serve mammon. It is not possible to jointly serve God and personal desire with equal attention. Serving God supersedes every other thing in life. However it requires wisdom of God and understanding to do this rightly.

This suggests that it is self-deceit to pretend to serve God and at the same time pay attention to something else.

Where then is the wisdom in reckoning with icons or obligatory regulations and commandments of men in the service of God (Col. 2:20–23)? Reason out the answer yourself.

Even God considered the use of stringed instruments as a purported means of praising Him as a mammon (Amos. 6: 5).

Yet men promote it above ministry of the gospel of Jesus crucified and above praise worship without stringed instruments but with what man has received from God; namely members of the body only. Caution is required in the service of God otherwise man may be worshipping mammon and think he is serving God.

It is important to watch out for possible derailment from true worship of God by the use of any man made things. Nowadays such things abound in the service of God. The impact has been both positive and negative. This is the challenge faced by all who patronise these things. These things are best apt to bring about laughter and to strengthen the physiology and the heart of the earthly man and gladden his life (Ps. 104:15).

But the satisfactions they provide are less important in the worship of God. Over indulgence in merry making through dance to stringed instruments might impinge on required attention to the word of God which then suggests the worship of mammon. So it is important to take care of how, and to what extent a believer desires to be a partaker of the material things of other people (1 Cor. 9:7–14). It may become a service to mammon when a bondservant sets his mind on earthly things to the detriment  of dedicating his time and energy and resources to minister the word and prayer (Acts 6:4). So there is need for the boundary of separation between the use of material things to the advantage of God and the drift into the desire of the flesh to be clear in our mind. Giving attention to earthly things has the potential to hinder the gospel of Christ. Chances are that it might give an opportunity to somebody who may desire the opportunity to be regarded as 'he who pays the piper dictates the tune' (2 Cor. 11:12).It was to guard against this banana peel that Paul laboured with his hands for his livelihood to avoid mixing the things of stomach with the gospel of Jesus crucified (2 Thes.3:8). Paul relied on his handwork for our learning (1 Thes. 2:9).

The trickery of mammon is evident in the service of God. Paul aptly recognised this and left examples for every bondservant of Jesus to follow.

This is one aspect of the life of Apostle Paul which requires all to imitate in the same way he too imitated Jesus (1 Cor. 11:1). Jesus Himself imitated God the Father according to the scriptures.

This suggests that to serve God is teamwork between like minds as brothers, without any working alone. The scripture has made it known that man cannot serve God and mammon at the same time (Mt. 6:24). This suggests that the desire for gain through manmade doctrine of material prosperity might indeed be a service to mammon (1 Tim. 6:5).

There is no doubt that whatever is of mammon is an addition to the scriptures, which is in contrast to the word of God (Rev. 22: 18–19). Therefore it is more beneficial to the gospel to labour for one's own livelihood outside the labour in the vineyard of God. Then make friends with earthly things so earned, that when you die people who benefitted and have gone before you will give you a rousing welcome to eternity (Lk. 16:9).

Money in the service of God

The scriptures recognise that money answers all things (Eccl. 10:19; Prov. 10:15). With money, wine and oil and bread, which respectively gladden the heart, make the face shine and the heart strong, can be within reach (Ps. 104:15).

But the danger of having confidence in it is that it can dwarf the desire to seek the knowledge of the true life of God. Jesus identified money as mammon (Lk. 16:11) and the love of it as evil (1 Tim. 6:10).

But it is good for making friends in the world to come (Lk. 16:9).

The place of money under the law

Under the law money, as it is known today, was not popular. But in its place were farm products. It was out of this produce that the payment of 10% tithe was made obligatory for eleven tribes of Israel who were giving land as inheritance. The tithe was paid to the priests of the Levite  tribe as her own inheritance. Out of it, she too paid 10% tithe to God, which He however gave to Aaron (Num. 18:26–29). Moses borrowed the principle of tithing from the tithe paid by Abraham to Melchizedek long before the law was given (Gen. 14:20).

Levite priest

Obligatory giving of the tithe by Israel to the Levite priests in obedience of the law of Moses was in order

This man, as a Levite, has the right to make this demand because tithing was his ineritance under the law of Moses (Num 18:21). However, inheritance was forbidden to be transferred between tribes (Num 36:9).

The place of money under grace

The lack of knowledge has made money look like a source of confidence in the service and worship of God by faith. As a result, money has now given rise to a very worrisome challenge in truly seeking the kingdom of God and His righteousness (Mt. 6:33). The main problem seems to be the inability to draw the line between frivolous use of money and the proper utilisation of it in the service of God.

Money is mammon and it belongs to the world system. Jesus drew a clear divide between the divine and mammon when He declared that what is Caesar's be given to Caesar, and to give to God what belongs to Him (Mt. 22:21).

This suggests that much ado about money in local churches and elsewhere in Christianity is a disservice to the gospel of grace.

There is no doubt that money plays a very important role in effective evangelism for those who walk worthily as wardens of God (3 John 5–6, 8). This is when money is used as a tool and not to attract distraction (Mt. 6:19–21).

However, it is of concern that several 'men of God' come up with various trickeries to deceive even scholars. As a result they emphasise that a man needs to first sow material seed as a condition to receive the blessing of God. They adduce cunningly compelling justifications to first sow seed of material nature and to pay a tithe of 10% as a condition to get God to respond to prayer and desires.

As it has been shown, tithing was peculiar to the Levites and it was not to be transferred to any other tribe (Num. 36:9). *Therefore nobody should hide under it to demand tithe in the gospel of grace.*

The payment of tithe by Abraham to Melchizedek was voluntary and a one-off offer. It was not a continual exercise and it was paid for all his descendants who were then in his loins (Heb. 7:9). So as all men died in the loins of Adam, even so all the seeds in the loins of Abraham paid tithe once and for all time to Melchizedek.

Indeed, Melchizedek was the shadow of the Most High Priest, Jesus Christ, who is the substance and has come to man personally (Col/ 2:17).

As a result things that were of shadow have faded out of reckoning in the gospel of grace. These things include tithe, ark of tabernacle and so on.

True preacher preaches free message of Jesus crucified without putting a yoke on the audience.

Audience gives unconditionally. (Prov. 11:24–25)

In the gospel of grace Jesus finished all things which needed to be done to save man, but cut it short in (complete) righteousness (Rom. 9:28). Hence the soul and body have not been adorned with the investiture of righteousness and holiness, as it has been done to the new creation Spirit (Eph. 4:24).

This suggests that any form of coaxing people to sow material seed or pay tithe or any other demand is a subtle confession of unbelief in the finished work of Jesus (John 19:28–30). It suggests the rebuilding of that which Jesus has once fulfilled, and therefore making oneself a transgressor (Gal. 2:18). This is, in addition, to put a yoke of burden which no one has ever been able to carry on brethren (Acts 15:10).

The work in the service of God is void of competition and so number of members of flock does not matter but the sincere devotion to fishing for lost souls matters. One soul saved by anybody is enough credit to him.

Now the inheritance of the priest of the gospel of grace is not earthly things but an eternal life (John 17:3).

Chapter Twenty-Six

Testimony of True Worship

True worship of God is done within, in spirit and truth (John 4:24). The tint of it can be observed outwardly in the way a man conducts himself.

Worship is conducted in the spirit realm because God is Spirit and He dwells in the spirit realm in the likeness of light which nothing can approach (1 Tim. 6:16).

So to truly worship Him, man will have to be in the same spirit realm. It is there alone that truth is found, and where the heart can be made clean by the word of God (John 15:3). This suggests that it is the heavenly man, who is hidden in the earthly man that makes the connection to God in the spirit realm. This inward man is the one whom God can make to have wisdom, and so He desires truth from him (Ps. 51:6).

In the meantime, the worldly man lives on earth in iniquity (Ps. 51:5). But both the heavenly and earthly men are in cohesion. So both have to be still, quiet and patiently wait and submit to the still-small voice from within (1 Kings 19:11–14).

So in preparation to pray, let the mind of the outward man keep away from any thought regarding his environment – neither think of bread, nor work, nor anything else. Instead subject the mind to ruminate on the awesome power of God, and the several wonderful things He has done for you. Equally, keep the body quiet: no talking and no gyrating; instead listen more to the inner man and maintain self-control (James 1:19).

As a result the deed of the body, which is usually due to indiscipline, is put to death. This put the body in subjection to the righteousness of Jesus Christ (1 Cor. 9:27). As a result sin will lose hold of the man. Now let the mind be turned toward the life in the realm of the Spirit of God where the evil spirit cannot enter. This keeps all conscious thoughts about earthly issues frozen in quietness and stillness of the heart. Then the outward man will join the inner man to wait on the Lord (Ps. 25:5). This is the moment that the man surrenders his spirit to the Spirit of faith, or the Spirit of God. It is an indication of man's faith in Christ Jesus (Heb. 11:1).

This unseen seeking of notice by man is what is known as the 'deep calls to deep'.

Now that the man is in the spirit realm with God, he is able to confess his desires and to seek deliverance, and then be raised above his foes (Ps. 42:7). As a result God might incline to the man and hear his cry (Ps. 40:1).

The instrument of governance of the wisdom of God (faint beam in the sketch) will produce the imprint of light in the divine heart in the kingdom of God within man (Lk. 17:21). It is the imprint that has been decoded to man as grace. It is by it that the God who commanded light to shine out of darkness will shine in the heart of man to reveal the knowledge of the glory of God in the face of Christ (2 Pet. 1:9). This is through the prophetic word of the light, which shines in dark places.

Wisdom of God

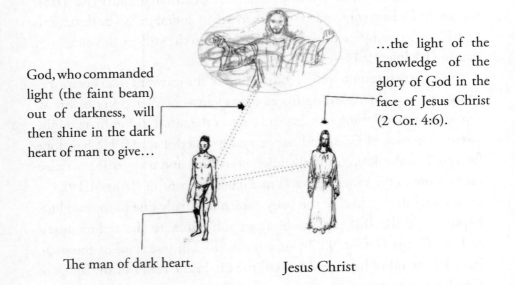

God, who commanded light (the faint beam) out of darkness, will then shine in the dark heart of man to give…

…the light of the knowledge of the glory of God in the face of Jesus Christ (2 Cor. 4:6).

The man of dark heart.

Jesus Christ

This is the knowledge which by grace equips man with the spirit and truth.

The light through the word will then awaken the consciousness of man within his dark heart and open it to behold the glory of God and believe (Acts 16:14). It is only then that man can truly worship God for His good pleasure (Phil. 2:13).

However, a man at this point still has the choice to believe or not. The man who chose to believe will become a vessel by which Christ Jesus, and not him, preaches the gospel for the sake of God (2 Cor. 4:5). This suggests that man has nothing to boast of in the work of the gospel of grace, or Jesus crucified (Gal 6:14).

It is only by the teaching of the Holy Spirit that man will read the word of God to understand. Any self-effort will lead to wrong interpretation, which may conceal the hidden things of shame. As a result man may not be able to discern the truth and escape totally from the condemnable attractions of earthly life (Gal. 5:19–21).

The man who worships God by the power of Christ, as shown earlier, will display the earthly virtues of divine nature which are the fruit of the Spirit (Gal. 5:22–23).

When the inner man is in submission to God the outward man is quiet in agreement. As a result he may not be aware of his surroundings because he will be weighed down by his surrender to the soul. This might even cause him to cry profusely in silence. This suggests that rowdiness is a far cry from the true worship of God, and it is not even germane for praise worship.

Difference between old and new worship

Introduction

The old way of worship relied on making of sacrifices with the blood of animals. So Jesus first took away the old covenant which established the animal sacrifice system. To accomplish this Jesus first accepted to be the sins committed by man, and to admit the guilt and bear the punishment. Then in theory He set up the new covenant with His blood at the last supper (Heb. 10:9). This was later sealed by the shedding of the blood of Jesus by crucifixion on the tree of the body which God had prepared for the purpose. It was sacrifice which was done once to cover every sin ever committed forever for those who are being sanctified (Heb. 10:12, 14).

This is the background of the proclamation of "it is finished" by Jesus on the cross. It signified the end to the practice of sacrifice of animal blood for the remission of sins (Heb. 10:18). This completely fulfilled the law of Moses forever.

On the other hand, it gave approval to the new worship of God by faith (Mt. 27:57–60).

Even though some people continued with animal sacrifice until a later date, it was of no significance. However, the new order of worship took root and began to evolve from the moment Christ Jesus arose from the dead (Mt. 28:6)

The three days' suspense between the burial of Jesus and the resurrection of Christ described the gap between the old and the new order of worship.

Jesus died in place of all men as it was prophesied by Caiaphas, the high priest of the time, that the world might be saved (John 11:50). This clearly shows why all should avoid a mix of the old and the new in every area of the gospel of Jesus crucified (Mt. 9:16–17).

The practitioner of worship under the law is the human being, and under grace he is the spirit being.

The features of old worship under the law

Under the law worship takes the form of physical activities and every aspect was done in a set process. Shedding of animal blood, use of incense to sanctify things, use of grain and wine and so on for sacrifices, and various washing ceremonies.

A material known as ephod was used to make enquiry of the Lord (1 Sam. 30:7). All these services were performed before the shadow of the heavenly ark of tabernacle on earth. It symbolised the point of contact with the invisible God (Ex. 25:40). The priest and prophets played the role of the spiritual messengers of the Lord to the people. The priest alone received the authority to offer sacrifices for himself first, and then for the people (Heb. 5:3). Also, only the priest had the right to enter the Holy of Holies (Heb. 9:7), read the Bible, and baptise with holy oil anointing (1 Sam.16:21).

The priest alone (apart from fools) was fearless. Worship was centralised and done only at the temple in Jerusalem where the ark of tabernacle, as the symbol of the unseen God, was situated Deut. 12:15, 11; Jer. 3:16).

The scope of the worship attracted obligatory requirements like tithing according to the law of Moses, fasting by abstinence, dedication of things to God, various ceremonies of washing and several other practices with material things (Mt. 23:23).

To obey the Ten Commandments was sacrosanct, and so were ceremonial laws and regulations, which were crafted on the command of God (Ex. 15:26).

The features of new worship by faith

Under grace the Lord Jesus Christ is the sole mediator. In the true worship of God every worship is done with what man has received from God (the word, lips, tongue, bare hands, et al). Now Jesus is Spirit under the gospel of grace, and He is so regarded by His disciples (2 Cor. 5:16). The worship of God is by faith through Christ.

Every believer is described as a saint and a priest by virtue of Christ (1 Pet. 2:9). So he is equally regarded as spirit like Christ. This suggests that his focus is on things of God above and not on issues of stomach or issues of table (Acts 6:4).

Here worship is done in Spirit and truth by both faith and the intrinsic work in the voice of faith in any physiological position and everywhere (John 4:24). This suggests that the attitude to life of a believer is visibly observed to be different from what is the norm in the world of man (Acts 11:26). The message of grace is centred solely on Jesus crucified (1 Cor.1:23; 1 Cor.2:2). Everybody is free to worship according to their own choice, but steadfast on Jesus for him who chose life (Deut. 30:19). All things are done in love of brothers, as demonstrated by Jesus Christ (1 John 4:11-12). Disciples imitate Apostle Paul in conduct, as he too imitated Jesus (1 Cor. 11:1).

Chapter Twenty-Seven

The Power of Grace

The loss of sight and hearing, and their restoration by Jesus

At creation God made man to hear His voice and that of all that He created. So man was able to relate with every creature. Even though he was naked he was not ashamed (Gen. 2:25) because he was clothed with the glory of God (2 Cor. 5:1). But after he disobeyed God the glory disappeared. Then he noticed that he was naked, for he seized to see and hear the voice of creation. As a result, he was ashamed.

This suggests the origin of the blindness and deafness of man. Thereafter man lived with a dull heart in addition to his alienation from the wisdom, knowledge and understanding of God. Then he began to grope as darkness in the noonday like a blind man gropes in darkness (Deut. 29:28–29).

As a result of this frustration man began to seek the Lord with the hope of finding Him. In the process he changed the glory of God to the image of creatures and the works of his hands (Acts 17:27; Rom. 1:23). It is in this state of hopelessness that man is conceived and born on earth (Ps. 51:5).

The woe of Israel, whom God chose later as His people, was multiplied by the law of Moses because they were unable to obey it as required.

The choice of Israel by God is what is actually an unmerited favour, and not grace. Rather, grace is a divine virtue which is the function of the Spirit of God and of glory.

For God to redeem His name He demonstrated His just righteousness by executing His foreordained plan to save man by grace. This resulted in the crucifixion of Jesus, that through His atonement God might be the justifier of the man who has faith in His Son (Rom. 3:26).

It set the recovery plan for the lost sight and hearing for the man who chose
to obey the plea of God to believe in Jesus Christ, that he might be saved and
restored from all the sins and curses that were previously committed (Rom. 3:25).

Righteousness and faith and the grace connection
Grace came through Jesus (John 1:17)

First, God shone in the dark heart of man (2 Cor. 4:6).

God's light gives light of the knowledge of the glory of God to shine in the face of Christ (2 Cor.4:6).

BI-5: It gives man access by faith to stand in grace. Then the reign of Christ manifests through him as a mere vessel to show the power of God (Rom. 5:2-5). This suggests walking in spirit (2 Cor. 5:16).

BI-I: Sinful man of darkness, blind and deaf with stony and dark heart (Deut. 28:28–29; Ps. 51:5).

B1-2: The knowledge enables man to believe in Jesus. Then God reckons it to him for righteousness (Rom. 4:5).

Heaven
Shower of gifts

(+)

Righteousness
Faith
Grace

JC

BI-3: God next gives the gift of the Spirit of faith to the man, that he might have own faith (Rom. 4: 20–21).

B1-4: The man's faith will be his surrender to the voice of the Spirit of faith. This is to deny one's own identity and take up Christ's identity. Being Christlike by faith is the justification to be co-heir with Christ. Then he will have peace with God through Christ (Rom. 5:1; James 4:7).

This suggests the process which might be followed to make man profit from the finished works of Jesus.

In which case the man shall remain blind and deaf and the inevitable end result is the second death or alienation from God forever (Rev. 21:8).

The foundation of the true gospel of grace

The only true gospel is that of Jesus crucified (1 Cor. 2:2). The crucifixion of Jesus put an end to both the self-righteousness of the Gentiles and the righteousness of the law of Israel (Acts 2: 22–23). The resurrection of Jesus Christ formed the chief cornerstone of the gospel of grace. So the gospel is a stone of stumbling and a rock of offence. *Whoever falls on this stone will be broken; but on whomever it falls, it will grind him to powder* (Acts 4:10–11; Mt. 21:42, 44). This Jesus Christ, who is the resurrection, was rejected by mankind. But He became the chief cornerstone of the foundation of the gospel of grace, which Apostle Paul alone laid by the grace of God for our salvation (1 Cor. 3:10–11; Eph. 2:20).

Apostle Paul alone laid the foundation. This is what qualified him to be called 'father' in the gospel of grace in Christ (1 Cor. 4:15). So it is only Paul that is like Abraham, who is the father of faith.

This suggests that the gospel of grace is the cross of our Lord Jesus Christ. Therefore any man who believes in Christ has been crucified by the gospel to the world, and the world has equally been crucified to him (Gal. 6:14).

This testifies that the message of the cross is the power of God to the man who is being saved, but foolishness to the man who is perishing (1 Cor. 1:18). The man who has been crucified to the world by the message of the cross will not regard as worthy the regulations and Commandments of man.

This suggests that the gospel of grace alone might be the rightful reason for a true disciple of Christ Jesus to boast.

Chapter Twenty-Eight

The Marriage of Man to Christ

It was established in Chapter 2 that the soul is that which God created in His image and likeness, and called man in the beginning (Gen. 1:26–27).

This suggests the authoritative position of the scripture with regards to who you are. It is the reason Jesus declared that man should not fear who can kill only the body, but fear Him (God) who can kill both the body and the soul (Mt. 10:28).

The soul is not destructible because he is a piece of God.

But the old spirit of man which was previously shown to have been formed within him, the soul, and the body which is the outward man that was formed from the dust of the ground were subject to destruction. This was evident in the crucifixion of Jesus. On that occasion, both the body and spirit of man were annihilated for those who might believe in Jesus Christ (Rom. 6:5–6).

But the soul was not. Instead the soul of Christ, which God prepared especially for the sacrifice, was killed (Is. 53:10).

Illustration of the marriage arrangement

New creation Spirit(2 Cor. 5:16–18):
This Spirit is owned by Christ for man (Gal. 2:20). It is this Spirit that now receives the testimony of God to convert the soul to Christ (Ps 19: 7). Once the new creation is linked to man, he becomes wife to Christ as the husband. i.e: Soul of Gentile who previously lived in self-righteousness but now believes in Jesus. Soul of Israelite who previously lived in the righteousness of the law but now believes in Jesus.

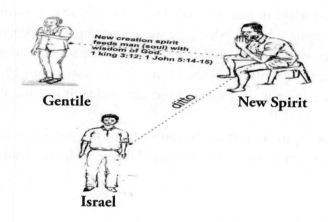

The foregoing text was to fulfil the requirement of the scripture of an eye for an eye (Ex. 21:24). Then God created a new Spirit in Christ for man. This is the Spirit which God now gives to whomever might believe in His Son (Gal. 2:20).

In the old arrangement the spirit was owned by man, the soul, according to the scripture (Zech. 12:1b).

God gave the spirit free will to scout for the soul. So he alone received the ability to covenant with the Spirit of God and the spirit of error. It was from whomever he tied himself to that he received wisdom and knowledge and understanding to feed the soul. It is this arrangement that described the marriage of the soul (man) as wife to the principal as the husband.

So when there was no law the Devil was the principal, which

arrangement began in the Garden of Eden. For Israel who received the law, the law was the principal for Israelites. However the Devil remained the principal for the Gentiles.

Now that the Spirit is owned by Christ, the soul who might believe in Christ will in hope be anchored in Him as the husband by the Spirit (Heb. 6:19).

The new Spirit in Christ for man was created in holiness and righteousness, and has been sealed by the Holy Spirit (Eph. 4:24; 30). So the Spirit cannot be corrupted. As shown in the illustration, the Spirit is who now links the soul who will believe in Jesus to Christ. Then the soul will become a slave of the righteousness of God in Him (Rom. 6:18). This is the marriage of man as a wife to Christ as husband (Rom. 7:4).

The foregoing shows that the new creation Spirit-man is the matchmaker who joins the soul-man to Christ. The soul is in the likeness of the branch and Christ is in the likeness of the vine (John 15: 4). As a result the soul-man will be able to produce good fruit to God by faith in Him (Gal. 5:22–23).

It is worthy to note that the soul-man of the would-be believer is currently being transformed to the same image of Christ Jesus (2 Cor. 3:18).

Chapter Twenty-Nine

Potency of Praise and Prayer

In the city of Philippi there was a slave girl with the spirit of divination. She used the power to deceive the people to make money for her master. Daily she harassed Apostle Paul and Silas by proclaiming them servants of God. So Paul cast the spirit out of her. In retaliation her master dragged them to the magistrate who ordered that they be beaten with rods and locked up in prison (Acts 16:13–34).

Then thrown into prison.

The executioner of the magistrate whipping Paul and Silas with the rod.

1. Feet fastened in the shoe.
2. They sang hymns and prayed.
3. Great earthquake occurred

Great earthquake occurred.

Keeper of prison

Paul and Silas set free.

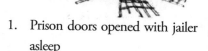

1. Prison doors opened with jailer asleep
2. Paul and Silas freed, but stayed.

The jailer was frightened to see the prison doors opened when he woke up, thinking the prisoners had escaped. Then he attempted to commit suicide, but Paul promptly called to assure him that they were around.

That the prisoners did not escape further baffled the jailer. Then he asked Paul what he must do to be saved. Paul told him to just believe in the Lord Jesus Christ. The jailer did, and he was saved with his household.

Afterwards the magistrates pleaded with Paul and Silas to depart from the city without further embarrassment, but with pleasantries (Acts 16: 27–39). This suggests that suffering and persecution and hate and humiliation are some of the evidence of the cross that must be carried daily as a disciple of Jesus. Nonetheless they constitute the weight of joy for being a partaker of the experience of Jesus in the service of God.

In all instances in which the wicked shows his pangs against the disciple of Jesus, the grace of God will always be available to him to overcome (2 Cor. 12:9).

An incidental benefit of experiencing the act of wickedness is that it might give an opportunity to win new converts to the faith.

The jailer struck a good example in the case of the experience of Paul and Silas in Philippi.

Chapter Thirty

The Lesson of Wide and Narrow Gates

The wide and narrow gates which Jesus identified denote the false and the true gospel respectively. The false gospel is preached by the wolves in sheep's clothing (Mt. 7:15). But the true disciples of Jesus preach only Him crucified (1 Cor. 2:2).

Feel-good message of glamour and promise of fortune and divination and profit with lip service to God (false message):

(1). Motivational doctrine. (2). Mixing of gospels of law and grace. (3). Vision of own imagination, but claimed to be from God and so makes listeners worthless (Jer. 23:16–17). (4). Show of signs and wonders on pulpit, but ignore the real sick people in public places. (5). Self-righteousness, material prosperity, fables, doctrines of fortune, etc. (2 Pet. 2:1–2; 1 Tim. 4:1–3).

Wide gate is an allegory for perverse gospel. viz:

These are messages which appeal to men of the world

The blind multitude in sin is drawn in vain (John 8:21) due to the bait of instant gain and lust of flesh and pride (1 John 2:16).

Broad way

But leads to broad way

Lake of fire (Place of torment)

Which leads to destruction (Mt. 7:13) – Lake of fire.

Synonymous with: The gospel of grace only, which is the message of Jesus crucified (1 Cor. 2:2; Gal. 6:14; 2 Timothy 4:2).

Narrow gate Mt. 7:14

Appeals to:
Only a few willing people will accept the truth (Lk. 13:24)

And it equally leads to:
Difficult and tortuous way to go (Mt. 7:14).

But leads finally to:

Eternal life of glory

The narrow gate leads to the difficult road (Mt. 7:14). The road ends in the salvation of the soul and also the end of faith (1 Pet. 1:9).

The prize of a successful journey through this road is the final investiture of righteousness of God in Christ upon the soul and body.

So the final destination (eternal life or hell) of man will depend on the personal choice to enter by either the narrow gate or the wide gate respectively.

The actions necessary to avoid being led astray from the pathway of truth along the tortuous road by false prophets who preach misleading and perverse gospel is what the scripture means by 'work out own salvation' (Phil. 2:12).

In walking this route every old way of life of self-righteousness or righteousness of the law becomes an undesirable burden and a drawback which must be abandoned. This includes but is not limited to every conduct (lie, falsehood, adultery, envy, murder, lust, eye for gain in the ministry of the gospel, etc.) which is an abomination to the Lord (Gal. 5:19–21).

The struggle to deny oneself of the entire old way of life is the cross which every person (he who believes in Jesus) carries daily (Lk. 9:23).

This suggests that the race requires every participant to have a pure heart and undefiled body to make meaningful progress. To achieve this objective might attract the burden of the cross. This includes hate, name-calling, persecution, envy, deliberate deprivation of entitlement, possible frame-up by people of contrary views, trials, perseverance and the like. So be contented with what is available to you and learn to abound in plenty and in famine, giving thanks to God always (Phil. 4:12).

This is to empty oneself to God, and to realise that it is the Lord who supplies the need of man to him. This is irrespective of the status of the individual in life (James 1:17). The gospel of grace is contrary to desiring earthly things besides the basic need of life (Acts 6:4). This attitude is not a call to poverty in any way.

The man who walks the difficult way gives himself up in prayers and thanksgiving to God always. He regards everything he receives as a gift from the Lord (Phil. 4; 16, 19). So in everything that has an option of choice in which God is involved, he makes the affairs of the kingdom of God his first choice. This is putting God first (Lk. 9:58–62).

Chapter Thirty-One

(A). Be an Ambassador of the Kingdom of God

God came down from heaven to earth in the form of man (1 Tim. 3:16). His objective was to set man free from the bondage of sin (Mt. 1:21; Mk. 1:38).

The man that Jesus came to save got into his beggarly form when he believed the serpent in the Garden of Eden when it claimed that he could be like God (James 1:14–15). The scripture symbolised his denial of God and the covenant with the Devil to eat the fruit of the knowledge of good and evil. In accord with the penalty God set for defiance, Adam surely has to die (Gen. 2:17).

Then God cast him out of Eden to grope at noonday as the blind man gropes in darkness (Deut. 28:29).

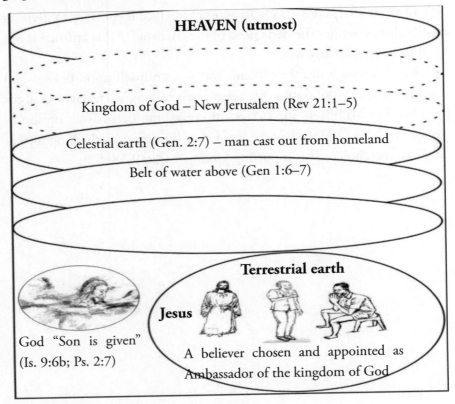

HEAVEN (utmost)

Kingdom of God – New Jerusalem (Rev 21:1–5)

Celestial earth (Gen. 2:7) – man cast out from homeland

Belt of water above (Gen 1:6–7)

Terrestrial earth

Jesus

God "Son is given" (Is. 9:6b; Ps. 2:7)

A believer chosen and appointed as Ambassador of the kingdom of God

Then man began to seek the Lord in the hope that he might grope for Him in the land of darkness and find Him (Acts 17: 27). But the search was in vain.

However God, for the sake of His name, saved all by grace through Jesus (Eph. 2:8). The Lord then reawakened in us the consciousness of the kingdom of God within man (Lk. 17:21). This is the outcrop of the real homeland of our heavenly man – the soul – bought with a price by the blood of Jesus (1 Cor. 6:20). It is the reason for man to be an ambassador of the Kingdom of God (2 Cor. 5:20).

(B). Be an ambassador of the kingdom of God

Citizen of kingdom of God (Jn. 17:14; Phil. 3:10). Preaches message of the kingdom of God only(Mt. 24:14).That is Jesus sacrificed (1 Cor. 2:2).

Key rudiments to be an ambassador:
• Every believer is given the Holy Spirit, which identifies him as a son of God in a similar manner to how Jesus was identified after water baptism (Mt. 3:16–17). Then he is called to be an ambassador.
• Lord Jesus similarly gave the Holy Spirit to His disciples to qualify them as sons of God (John 20:22).
• It was after that He commissioned them to the field to make disciples of all nations (Mt. 28:19).
• The ambassador is chosen and appointed by the benefactor king in case of disciples (2 Cor. 5:20).
• Ambassador is not self-appointed but by God, who equally chose the priest under the law (Jer. 3:15).
• Ambassador represents the interest and not the person of God. So he is not to please man but God (Col. 2:20–23).
• Ambassador is not to regard man as father in obedience to the word of God (Mt. 23:9), nor seek the honour of men (Jn. 5:42).
• Ambassador of the kingdom is a foreigner and pilgrim on earth, and obeys the laws of the land (Heb. 11:13).
• But he neither play local politics (2 Pet.2:20), nor engages in the business of the land (2 Tim. 2:4; Gal. 5:1).
• God freely adds all his daily needs to him for use (Mt. 6:33).

The terrestrial earth is populated by men born in iniquity and sin (Ps. 51:5).

This puts the job of ambassador of the kingdom of God in conflict with the existing schemes of men. This conflict includes politics, the desire for earthly prosperity, worries about earthly issues, and the like. This is not to disparage riches. Rather it is to show that the things of the kingdom of God are at variance with the things of men and they are not to be mixed. Ambassador is freely supplied with his material need by God (Mt. 6:33b).

In all considerations an ambassador must put God first. This might make you odd in the eyes of worldly people.

Surely it may attract envy, hate, persecution, tribulation, name-calling, desertion by fair-weather friends, and so on (John 6:66).

The ambassador is to imitate Apostle Paul in a similar way to that in which he too imitated Jesus Christ (1 Cor. 11:1).

In this way he builds on the foundation laid by Apostle Paul with eternal materials (1Cor. 3:10-15).

The materials include: to adhere to prayers and ministry of the gospel of Jesus crucified only, give free services to the needy for the sake of God. Love all as God has first shown love to us through Jesus, do all things by faith in God and in hope of the crown of righteousness, do not build with straws such as messages of falsehood which is centered on earthly things, exploitation, and so on.

Most importantly, the ambassador must regard himself according to the spirit, similar to how Jesus Christ is now regarded according to the Spirit (2 Cor. 5:16).

This means that he does not belong to this earth any longer. He lives on earth to produce the fruit of the Spirit and win souls to the kingdom of God (Gal. 5:22–23).

This is to know that his citizenship is not of this world. It is a way to imitate Jesus whose kingdom is not of this world (John. 18:36).

An ambassador is a dependable believer in Christ with strength to endure and to do all things in love. So he is to bear and hope that all things will turn out to please God (1Cor. 13:7). This is the way to overcome mudslingers and men of contrary opinion (1 Cor. 13:7). He is to keep the mind focused on things in heaven, store spiritual treasures and regard old habits and desires as rubbish (Mt. 6: 19, 24–25; Phil. 3:7–8).

Get engaged with lawful activities that will not mortgage the boldness to defend the word of God, but will fetch you daily sustenance and give God avenue to add to meet your daily needs (2 Thes. 3:7–10; Mt. 6:33). Learn to abound in plenty and in famine (1 Pet. 3:17–18) and don't give man any opportunity to gag you and keep you from speaking the truth of the word of God at any time. So do not depend on man. But the ambassador is free to accept free gifts as a promoter of the gospel of the kingdom of God, and not because of poverty.

Let the hope of the reward of the crown of righteousness be your drive and tolerance. Be knowledgeable about the plan of God concerning the present perishing creation. Keep in view the new heavens and earth which God has already created, but are waiting to be revealed (Is. 65:17). Spread the news of God's plan regarding the two creations to your audience. This might make them to buy into setting their minds and pursuit on things above against the desire for acquisition of things of this world which are perishing (Rom. 8:21–25; 2 Pet. 3:10; Rev. 21:1–4).

As an ambassador, learn not to be haughty by thinking of oneself more as a mere vessel in the hands of God, to whom you should give all the glory (Rom. 12:3).

Chapter Thirty-Two

Covetousness

Covetousness happens in variety of ways. In many cases it may not be known that an error is being committed. But a careful read of the scriptures exposes every form of covetousness.

The finished work of Jesus on the cross has already secured all the treasures of God in the heavens and in the world in Him for man (Eph. 1:3). This suggests that every visible possession on earth belongs to somebody already.

That somebody might have received it from either God through Christ Jesus by faith, or without faith from the Devil through the works of darkness. This is because the Devil still lays claim to worldly things in the absence of Jesus Christ.

If possessions can be called up by faith, why then do believers need to work?

Believers work because God created man in the beginning for the purpose of managing the works of His hand in the Garden of Eden (Gen. 2:5, 15). While this relationship lasted, man looked unto God and created whatever he needed by spoken words and waited patiently till God responded by adding whatever he has desired to him. This was the way Adam created his needs.

Looking unto God suggests that Adam sought after the kingdom of God and His righteousness, in a similar manner to how Jesus has commanded man to do now (Mt. 6:33).

So to work is generally to do the will of God to complement His works (John 9:4). Additionally, it is an opportunity to manifest the talent which God has put in man.

It is work which makes it possible to practise the knowledge that man might have acquired by scholarship with the power which God has given to him to improve the human system, and thereby glorify His name (John 17:4).

So if a man desires to possess what already exists on earth, he has to follow the legitimate way to secure it. Then be ready to bear the consequences of the process adopted – God's way, or the Devil's way?

So to desire somebody's property without going through the due process is covetousness. It is the desire to be rich which leads to ruin that tempts man to go after anything unlawfully (1 Tim. 6:9–10). It suggests that to make an obligatory demand like tithing in the gospel of grace is a disguised covetousness. This is because the choice to part with what may have been received from God is of free will in the gospel of grace. So making a demand infringes on the individual's right, and therefore is illegal. It has the potential to hurt the benefactor to the gain of the beneficiary, in which case the receiver has not shown love as an image of God, who is love (1 John 4:7–13, 19–21).

Illustration of covetousness

Windows of heavens open to all who believe in Christ and first seek the kingdom of God and His righteousness (Mal. 3:10; Mt. 6:33a).

Flow of resources from the treasure of God to men who learn to do good, seek justice, rebuke the oppressor, defend the fatherless and plead for the widow (Is. 1:17) – (+)

Heaven

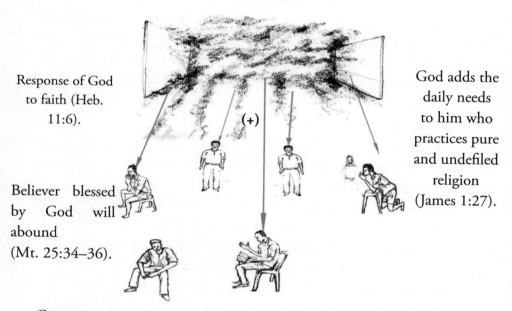

Response of God to faith (Heb. 11:6).

God adds the daily needs to him who practices pure and undefiled religion (James 1:27).

Believer blessed by God will abound (Mt. 25:34–36).

Covetous man sets mind on what another has received by faith from God (Lk. 16:14).

Believer who asks by faith receives (Mk. 6: 41–42; Phil 4:19).

Practical faith is equivalent to surrender to the Lord as the shepherd, and whoever does so will not want (Ps. 23:1).

Every observable possession of man has at one time or the other been called by somebody into existence by faith and then fashioned it into utility (Heb. 11:3). Exceptions are the natural things of God such as the primary physical features which man possesses by virtue of where he naturally found himself.

The wealth which a man has in his possession through the addition by God brings peace of mind to him, and he freely uses it to do the chosen fast of God. But the wealth which has been acquired without God comes with worries, fear, anxiety and bondage to the source of the treasures, and so on.

It is believed that such wealth turns the heart of man away from the Lord and instead blindfolds the owner to put trust in it (Mt. 19:22).

Manna does not fall from heaven anymore. Against this background there is the need for man to work to earn a living (2Thes. 3:6-10).

But do it as though you are doing it for the Lord (Col. 3:23–24). Once a man works with this mindset in whatever he does he will be putting God first and will unintentionally stand out as a model in the midst of people.

This is how to shine as light of God before men (Mt. 5:16).

It is this which inadvertently makes him the epistle of the gospel of grace to observers (2 Cor. 3:2).

As it has been seen, to work is to do the will of God, who then uses the avenue to fulfil His promise to add the needs of man (Mt. 6:33). This labour of man notwithstanding, it is God that feeds all, irrespective of personal efforts and the earnings attached (Mt. 6:25–34).

Thus the possession of anything by man is not in anybody's hands. This includes all who may appear to be larger than life, like the multipurpose and rich benefactors.

There is therefore no tenable reason for anyone to be covetous or boast.

Chapter Thirty-Three

Hardened Heart – A.1. (Mk. 3:5) and
Heart of flesh (believer) – B.1.

A.1. *The hardened heart seeks after earthly* **things…**

1. He justifies own opinion even when scripture says otherwise.
2. Regard gospel as means of gain.
3. Misread grace as favour.
4. Designs and preaches fantasy gospel of thrills (1 Tim. 4:1–3).
5. Duels on providing answers to desires of gain with false and exploitative words, quotes and divinations which he claims, falsely, to be from God (2 Pet. 2:3).
6. Focuses on building treasures on earth (Gen. 11:4).
7. Seeks self-interest and fame.
8. Denies God by the wilful sin of not preaching Jesus crucified, having received the knowledge of truth and tasted God's goodness and power (Heb. 6:4–6; Heb. 10:26, 29).

A.1.1. *…but ignores or pays lip service to:*

1. 1. Feat by God of past miracles and healing (Gen. 14:21; Mk. 5:34; Mt. 14:25) etc.
2. 2. The feeding of the multitude with five loaves of bread and two fishes (Mk. 6:42).
3. That Jesus alone gave Himself for our sins to save us (Gal. 1:4).
4. Testimony of the true and only desired gospel of Jesus crucified (Gal. 1:6–7).
5. What will happen to his soul after mortal death (Mt. 16:26).
6. Warnings about false prophets (Mt. 7:15), etc.
7. Confidence in the word of God which requires man to first seek God's kingdom and His righteousness, and that He will add man's earthly needs to him (Mt. 6:33)

B.1. Heart of flesh seeks after:

1. The kingdom of God and His righteousness (Mt. 6:33).
2. The truth: Jesus crucified (1 Cor. 2:2).
3. Winning souls to Christ by saying it as it is written (Mt. 4:19).
4. Producing fruit of Spirit (Gal. 5:22–23).
5. Show of love by giving, forgiveness (Rom. 12:9–10; Mt. 25:40).
6. Staying away from false preachers and doctrines (2 Pet. 2:1; Mt. 7:15),

B.1.1. Heart of flesh forgets and shuns:

1. The ugly past of self-righteousness (Phil. 3:8).
2. Every tradition associated with the ark (Jer.3:16) and law.
3. Any gospel different from that of Jesus crucified (Gal. 1:6-7).
4. Competition of all shades amongst 'men of God' (1 Cor.1:12–13) etc.

Things that will not defile man:

- What enters the body from outside will not defile the (soul) man (Mk. 7:15).
- Such ingested food, drink and medic drip do not enter divine heart but only journey within the outer man, and eventually eliminated (Mk. 7:19).
- Washing hands to eat is for the
- reason of hygiene only.
- Conversely, what a man takes in through the mouth cannot make the heart pure, which is the reason to fast.

Things that defile man:

- It is what comes from the heart of the inner man that defiles him (Mk. 7:15). These things pertain to what alienate man from God, which are things of iniquity and sin (Is. 59:2).
- Evil feelings: thoughts of adultery and fornication (Mt. 5:28), murder (Mt. 5:22), thieving, covetousness, wickedness, deceit, lewdness, an evil eye, blasphemy, pride, foolishness, lies, perversity, injustice, etc. (Is. 59:3).
- Therefore guard the tongue and restrain the mouth. (James 3:5–12).

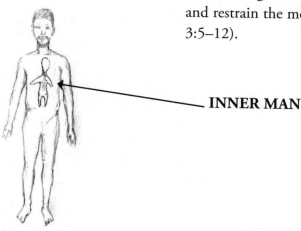

INNER MAN

BODILY MAN

1. The foregoing suggests that the soul is the man that is defiled by perversion of the perfect works of God with ungodly intentions.
2. Now the new creation Spirit has been sealed by the Holy Spirit, and therefore he cannot be defiled, but the soul can which suggests that he is the real man, or you (2 Cor. 1:22).
3. The earthly man only becomes a partaker because he plays the role of weapon of unrighteousness (Rom. 6:13). It is he who executes outwardly the hidden, evil intent of sex, murder, etc. This action of the outward man stains the soul because he gave thought to it and so leads to his defilement (1 Cor. 3:17).

Chapter Thirty-Four

Traits of Born Again and of Sinful Man

The man who later turned sinful was created upright in the beginning (Eccl. 7:29).

His woes began when he chose to believe the serpent, which was possessed by the Devil, against the command of God. *Thus disobedience gave life to sin in the life of man.* Adam, who committed the first sin in Eden, was weakened to the extent that he lost the ability to help himself. This suggests that to believe makes man a slave to what is believed. For this reason man has since been a slave to sin (Rom. 8:34).

Conversely, to believe in Jesus will equally lead man to be reconciled to God in the body of Jesus Christ through death, and to be a slave to His righteousness (Col. 1:21–23). What happens subsequently to make man become a new creation (born again) is entirely managed by the Holy Spirit. This suggests that to just believe in God and then receive prayer from a 'minister' does not make a man whose old features and behaviours remain intact an instant born-again. It is a lack of knowledge that makes people to think otherwise (Hos. 4:6). God alone sees the heart and adjudges who measures up to be given a new Spirit, which will cause an instant change of life and subsequent uprightness of soul and body.

Illustration

Sinful man (A)

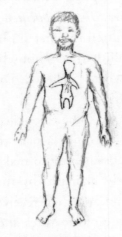

- Earthly man – no change of body, has own DNA.
- Old heavenly man (soul) – no change, has Adam's DNA.
- Old spirit of man –no change, has own DNA.

Self-righteous

- Earthly man – no change of body, has own DNA.
- Old heavenly man (soul), being renewed daily and washed to DNA of Christ (2 Cor.4:16; 3:38).
- Spirit of Christ of new creation in righteousness and holiness (Eph. 4:24); has God's DNA (2 Cor. 5:17–18, 21) and sealed by the Holy Spirit (2Cor. 1:22)

Born-again (B):

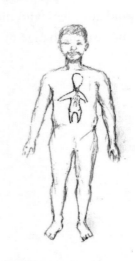

Believe in Christ

The distinction

New creation (born again)

- Spirit, soul and body are in unity and depend on God through Christ.
- The Spirit is owned by Christ, who gave him to man – the soul (Gal. 2:20).
- The Spirit is righteous and holy (Eph. 4:24) and he is anchored in Christ (Eph. 2:5–6).
- He is sealed by the Holy Spirit (Eph. 1:13–14) to guarantee the inheritance of the believer, until the salvation of the soul later (1 Pet. 1:9).
- So he cannot sin or be polluted (1 John 3:9).
- It is the Spirit that makes external contact with the Spirit of God only. This leads the soul to receive the God's wisdom, knowledge to act wisely (1 Cor. 12:4–6).
- This is how man is married to Christ (Rom. 7:4).
- So it is the Spirit which makes the fellowship of man with Christ possible.
- The soul is undergoing washing, or the regeneration and renewing of the Holy Spirit to become born again in the image of Christ (Titus 3:5b, John 3:3).
- Now the body is earthly, but at God's set time the Holy Spirit shall give him life and he will not be left as dust, but changed to a spirit body (John 8:11; 2 Cor.5:1).
- This is the resurrection of the body.
- The man who has received the new Spirit walks in Spirit (Gal. 5:16) by manifesting the fruit of the Spirit in his behaviour (Gal. 5:22–23).
- Seeks heavenly things (Mk. 10: 43–45). Hatred, persecution, etc. mean nothing to him (Lk. 14:26).

Sinful man

- Spirit, soul and body are in unity but independent of God.
- The spirit is owned by man (the soul). God made him within man (Zech. 12:1). The union of spirit and soul is nicknamed flesh to identify him as self-will and as another speaking spirit.
- It makes him prone to and conscious of sin. The spirit is the lifeline of the soul, and it is him that covenants with external sources on behalf of the soul. The spirit itself is seeking and lacks knowledge of God.
- The spirit married man (Israel) to the law and Gentiles to the Devil.
- The soul has the DNA of Adam (Gen. 5:3).

- The body is perverse and so will see corruption as dust in contrast to the fate of a believer in Jesus (Ps. 16:10). This means that the union shall awake to condemnation and everlasting torment (Dan. 12:2b).
- The man entangles himself with the old desires. So God gave him the work of collecting and gathering worldly things to keep him busy in vain (Eccl. 2:26b).

Chapter Thirty-Five

Let the Wise Imitate Jesus

It is Jesus alone that has come from and went back to heaven. In His mission on earth He laid much emphasis on the affairs of the kingdom of God. It is there that all who believe in Him are hoping to go someday. This makes it imperative to imitate His erstwhile conduct as an earthly man which we presently are.

Fortunately the scripture is awash with examples of the upright behaviour of Jesus for us to copy. This is replete in His teachings and conduct as it concerns every category of people which include religion, politics, the down trodden, and the general public (2 Tim. 3:16).

Although He did all this under the law, it was a futuristic lifestyle meant for man to imitate in due time, which is the post resurrection era (Mt. 22:1–14).

After Apostle Paul was converted he became the more familiar example of how to imitate Jesus (1 Cor.4:16; 11:1). This leaves man with no excuse for not knowing how to conduct himself as a disciple of Jesus Christ. Jesus was fully man and fully God when He was on earth, but He lived as man in the order of the first Adam (Phil. 2:6–7). This exactly fits the disciple, who is now as a spirit-man in an earthly body (2 Cor. 5:16).

So there was nothing Jesus did as a man that the believer will not be able to do. This provides a common platform for man to imitate Him in every way in the likeness of a man who is in the world, but not of this earth. Doing this will manifest the combined characteristics of both the natural and the spirit natures of man. This is the way for man to understand the teaching of Jesus as it concerned the parables and prophecy.

Once this is understood, the spiritual power of man will be awakened and attracted towards the life pattern that is obtainable in the kingdom of God.

After the resurrection of Jesus Christ He seized to be in the form of an earthly and to be regarded so. Rather He put on his nature of God, making Him entirely Spirit in form – Spirit, Soul and body (2 Cor.5:16).

At the same time, God made a provision for any man who might believe in Him to first experience a similar change within him (Rom. 6:4). This is the beginning of the new creation Spirit in the man who might believe in Him.

Therefore any man who believes in Jesus is in the likeness of the resurrection of Christ Jesus. As a result he is to regard himself as spirit, just as He is now on the right-hand side of God in heaven (1 John 4:17).

All that Jesus did as a man is now revealed and brought to our remembrance by the Holy Spirit (John 14:26). God even shows to man His way in dreams or visions, or through hunches (Job 36:8–11).

This is the source of strength and the discerning power of man to subject his human conduct to the likeness of heavenly behaviour. It is how to imitate Apostle Paul, who equally imitated Jesus Christ (1 Cor.11:1).

In practice, first gain the true knowledge of what belongs to God through the study and true reading of the scriptures against what belongs to the world of man. This is to cover every aspect of life: love, grace, faith, forgiveness, righteousness etc.

Then begin to give to God that which belongs to Him, and to the man of the world that which belongs to the world.

In this way man will begin to follow the tradition which Jesus established and avoid the mixture of old practices and doctrine with the new (Mt. 9:16–17). Until man is able to discern the two sides of the coin and to properly assign them, he will be deceiving himself and others in imitating Jesus.

As of now the mixture of lie and truth is in vogue amongst men. This is replete in the gospel and doctrine which are generally communicated by men of the faith. This mixture is more in vogue in the demand for seed-sowing, and in divination, fasting, tithing, healing and miracles, and so on.

The consequences of this wave of 'message of men' have been the near total abandonment of the real gospel of Jesus crucified, the consideration of the hell fire which lies ahead of whoever denies Jesus, and what may happen to the soul after earthly life.

Jesus opened the window of wisdom for man to note and ponder on the undesirable mixture of things of God with the things of man. So He spoke of the wide and narrow gate, the true and false prophets in sheep's clothing (Mt. 7:13–15) and giving to Caesar what belongs to Caesar and to God what belongs to God (Mk. 12:17).

The onus is now on the individual to identify, separate and treat the content of every mixture on its merit.

Apostle Peter showed us an example when he distanced himself from the issues of serving the table. Rather, he chose dedication to prayer and ministry of the word of God (Acts 6:4). Apostle Paul was not different as he too was an epitome of self-denial for the sake of the true gospel. He loathed ungodly pleasures and endured persecution and inconvenience. He risked his life to preach the true gospel in the face of hatred, beating, desertion by trusted men, and so on.

This is what is required of man to imitate Jesus. It suggests that doing anything which was not popular with Apostle Paul or Jesus is contrary to the gospel of grace.

In imitating Jesus, the first question to ask is, were Jesus and Apostle Paul preoccupied with the following practices? Ten per cent tithing, or fasting by abstinence, or dedication of things to God in their gathering, or preaching any gospel than that of Jesus crucified, or seeking their own worldly gain, or sowing to get material benefit in return, or building edifice for worship, and so on? Be wise my brethren in Christ. Be wise.

Every man is his own judge. He may justify what he is doing now or learn to accept the truth, which will ever remain the truth. Surely we shall all face the judgment Seat of Christ Jesus on the day which God has appointed for it (2Cor. 5:10). The choice is your'.

Chapter Thirty-Six

The Great Tribulation

The examination

In lamentation over Jerusalem, Jesus foretold the great tribulation which will be the mother of all tribulations. He reflected on the killings by Jerusalem of the prophets and those whom God had sent to rescue her in the past (Mt. 23:37; 2 Chr. 36:15–16). Then He foretold the ruin of the temple at Jerusalem (Mt. 24:2).

Jesus went on to narrate the events of the great tribulation. Worthy of note is that Jesus revealed for tidiness of reading that the persecution of Israel and the saints will happen first before the catastrophe. It clearly shows that all who will be alive will experience the great tribulation. But He assured us that the man who endures to the end will be saved (Lk. 21:12).

In heaven, God premeditated and settled the events of the great tribulation.

The scheme was unfolded in the throne room of heaven. The Most High God held out in His right hand the scroll sealed with seven seals, for anybody to open and remove the seals and read (Rev. 5:1; Ezek. 29:9–10). But there was nobody worthy to open the scroll or loosen its seals (Is. 29:11–12).

Then the Lamb on the throne volunteered to do it. On His removing the first seal it revealed a conquering and to conquer rider, which suggests the everlasting conqueror, or Christ Jesus, on a white horse (Rev. 6:2). *It suggests the second coming of the Lord Jesus to vanquish the perpetrator of the great tribulation – Satan.*

The removal of the rest of the six seals revealed the following, in the sequence shown:

i. *The authority to take peace from earth, which corroborates Jesus' prognosis of the talk of wars and rumour of wars that will precede the great tribulation (Mt. 24:6);*

ii. *a pair of scales, which symbolised Jesus' forecast of strife among nations and among kings, and also famines (Mt. 24:7);*

iii. *authority to kill a quarter of the earth with sword and hunger and death and the beast of the earth; and*

iv. *the souls of the killed faithful arrayed in white robes*

v. *a great earthquake and turmoil upon the inhabitants of the earth; and lastly*

vi. *seven angels, and trumpets given to each (Rev. 6:2–4, 6–8, 9–12, 16; 8:2).*

The contents of the seals represented two things:

1. The fate of the saints killed because of Jesus or His name.
2. The catalogue of unprecedented calamity which God has predetermined for this sinful earth during the great tribulation

This gives an indication that the turmoil will scare the life out of all those living on earth. All those alive will hide from the face of God and Christ and will seek to die instead of the ordeal, but death will not come to them.

In the plan, God has granted the four angels now bound in the river Euphrates the power to harm the earth and sea. However, He has put a restriction on them until 144,000 of His servants, all of the tribes of Israel, are sealed (Rev. 7:3). This suggests that the 144,000 servants of God will be in the form of man during the tribulation. They will pioneer the service to the Lord during the one thousand years' reign of the Lord Jesus on earth. In a similar way, the saved souls will serve God (Rev. 7:15; 22: 3).

This suggests that the Lord Jesus will not again take up the form of sinful man to be on this sinful earth during the thousand years. But He will dwell in the New Jerusalem which will be established afterwards in the imminent new earth (Rev. 21:3). However, the Lord Jesus will be in the clouds during the one thousand years' reign. God will provide a cover of cloud and smoke by day and the glow of a flaming fire by night over every assembly and home of His servants on this earth during the one thousand years' reign of Christ (Is. 4:5–6).

It further suggests that the men whom the Lord Jesus gave gifts before He ascended to heaven in His first coming (Eph. 4:11) will have completely perverted the gospel of Jesus crucified, and might have lost their relevance (1 Cor. 2:2).

The current event on earth: the saints preach the gospel of grace and Israel (the Jews) account for the things of the altar within the temple in current Jerusalem. But in the scheme of God, He has given the outer court, which has the gateway facing north, to the Gentiles (Rev. 11:2b; Ezek. 40: 20). This is to pave way at the appointed time for the army of the kings from the north to join forces with Satan.

They will enter and trample the holy city of Jerusalem that is now underfoot for three and a half years (Rev. 11:2). During this period the saints will flee to the wilderness where God has prepared a place for them, far away from the reach of the antichrist (Rev. 12:6).

The early years that will lead to the great tribulation will present peace and safety and economic boom. The prince of man who will later reveal himself as the antichrist will be accepted first by the people. But before then he will enter into covenant with Israel for a time. The period shall witness the revival of sacrifices and offering at the temple. However, midway into the romance, the concession and power shall be unilaterally shattered by the prince (Dan. 9:27).

Then the prince will turn out to be a beast with seven camouflaged heads. *This will be the observable, harsh beginning of the great tribulation.* Then he will begin to show his fangs and speak blasphemies (Rev. 13:5).

The beast will at a certain point claim to be God, and he will stand at the holy place of the temple. He will disregard all things, even the Most High God. That will be the height of the tribulation (Mt. 24:15; Lk. 21:22).

But as it has been established previously, it is God who has predetermined these happenings for the beast (Dan. 11:36). So he will accomplish them fully, irrespective of resistance by the saints and Israel.

At some point his head (one of the seven) will be wounded, but it will be healed miraculously. The world will marvel and be drawn to him.

Still Satan, who gave his great power and throne and authority to the beast, will be enraged. So he will make war with those who will keep the commandments of God and have the testimony of Jesus Christ (Rev. 12:7).

Another beast will perform incredible signs and wonders which have never been seen before. This beast will cause men on earth to make an image of the beast which was wounded and healed. Then he will give breath to the image and cause men to worship it, with the threat that whoever fails to do so will be killed.

He will cause all to receive the mark of the beast on their right hand or on their foreheads. No one may buy or sell without the mark, which is 666 (Rev. 13:11–17).

The Gentiles (ungodly), which the enemy king will lead, shall now trample upon Jerusalem. Many people shall be led away captive to all nations until the times of the Gentiles (ungodly) are fulfilled (Lk. 21:24).

In the meantime there will be deceit by false prophets, and betrayal by blood relations. Persecutions, trials, brutality, imprisonment and other tribulations, all of which will assume the level that have not been seen in the past, will be a common thing (Lk. 21:12, 16–17).

However, Jesus will uphold those who will believe in Him (Lk. 21:13–15, 18).

In spite of the chaos the gospel of the kingdom of God will be preached in all nations of the world as a witness to all, and then the end will come (Mt. 24:14).

It is for this purpose that the angel of the thrones of judgment will give power to his two witnesses dressed in sackcloth. They will prophesy for forty-two months (three and a half years) concerning the testimony of Jesus, which is the spirit of prophecy (Rev. 19:10b; Lk. 24:27). The men will equally testify of the flying scroll, which is the curse that goes out over the face of the whole earth to consume the evil ones (Zech. 5:3–4).

The witnesses symbolise the two olive trees and the two lamp stands which stand before the God of the earth. These represent the anointed ones who have the word of the Lord to Zerubbabel, which has declared: *Not by might nor by power, but by My Spirit* (Zech. 4:6, 14). This suggests that they will have the power of the Lord to let out fire from their mouths to destroy any man who will attempt to harm them (Rev. 11:4–5).

At the end of their prophecy the beast which will ascend out of the bottomless pit will make war against the witnesses, prevail and kill them (Rev. 11:7). Their dead bodies will be left to be in the street for three and a half days and will not be allowed to be buried.

But after three and a half days the breath of life from God will enter them. Then they will stand on their feet. Fear will grip those who will see it. But the witnesses will be called to heaven, and will then be caught up in the clouds to the surprise of the watchful eyes of their enemies (Rev. 11:11–12).

Earthquakes will destroy one tenth of the holy city and will kill seven thousand numbers of people. This will make the remnant left give glory to God of heaven (Rev. 11:13).

> *Israel will then believe in the Son of God and all will at*
> *that moment be saved (Is. 59:20-21).*

Then the predetermined events which were examined previously will begin to take place on earth with rapidity. People will hear of wars, and rumours of wars. Nations will war against nations, and kingdoms against kingdoms (Mt. 24:6–7). The general commotion will be intense (Lk. 21:10).

In addition, there will be famine, pestilence, fearful sights and great signs from heaven. Also, there will be great earthquakes in various places (Lk. 21:11).

The signs and second coming of Lord Jesus

The day the Lord shall come will be like in the day of Noah. On the day, Noah was ignorant of what might happen next after he heeded the command of God to prepare the ark. Other men ate and drank, they married wives, and they were given in marriage. The day came that Noah and the remnant which God chose entered into the ark. Then of a sudden, the flood came and floated the ark (Lk. 17:26–27).

The rest of the people who did not take the command of God seriously, and every other thing which Noah left behind, were destroyed (Gen. 7:19–23). It is in like manner that the great tribulation will range on like a game to the beast and false prophet and their allies. They will preach peace and safety to the persecuted but suddenly destruction will come upon them (1 Thes. 5:2–3).

Then there will be great signs in the firmament of heaven and on earth (Lk. 21:25). Like Noah, those who heeded the call of God to believe in Jesus will be ready for the Lord, as were the wise five virgins (Mt. 25:1–13). But all will be gripped with the fear of not knowing what is going to happen to them next (Lk. 21:26).

Then all of a sudden, there will appear signs of the Son of Man in the clouds. All persons shall see Him coming down on the clouds of heaven, with power and great glory (Mt. 24:30; Lk. 21:27; Dan. 7:13–14; Rev. 1:7). The tribes on earth will mourn borne out of either joy for those who believed, or regret for those who despised Jesus. He will descend on a white horse and a great multitude will follow Him, also on white horses (Rev. 19:11, 14).

This will be the ultimate sign that the kingdom of God is really near.

All of a sudden God will release fire from His mouth to immobilise the beast (prince). Then the beast will be captured and cast alive into the lake of fire.

The false prophet, who will work signs to deceive the people that will receive the mark of the beast (number 666) and worship his image, will also be cast alive into the same lake of fire (Dan. 7:11; Rev.19:20).

The Lake of Fire (Mt. 24:41)

The beast   **The Prophet**

The lake of fire

The rest of the army who will join the beast and the prophet to execute the great tribulation will be killed with the sword, which shall proceed from the mouth of the Lord (Rev. 19:21).

This will be the end to the great tribulation.

> *Then an angel will go forth to fish out twelve thousands from each of the twelve tribes of Israel. They will make up the 144,000 servants of God that will be sealed, as previously alluded to (Rev. 7:3). In addition the believers will not be harmed in the next sequence of calamities of the Seventh seal upon the element of earth. The believers will be protected by their prayers which will be offered to God by the angels (Rev. 8:3-5).*

This suggests that it might be during the same period of sealing the men that the saints chosen by God will be suddenly taken up from amongst their companions (Lk. 17:34–36). Reference: the harvest in Chapter 37 (so-called rapture).

The woe on the allies of Satan – day of vengeance (Is. 34:8)

Now the taking up of the chosen saints has taken place as previously seen.

In spite of the calamity which the people have witnessed, the rest of mankind will not repent of their evil conduct. They will continue to worship demons and idols of the handiwork of men, commit murders, sexual immorality and sorceries, and so on. (Rev. 9:20–21).

Then the seventh seal will be opened. This will be after the first resurrection. It suggests why the second death will not have power over them (Rev. 20:6).

The seven angels, of the seventh seal, which have a trumpet each, will be set free. They will be permitted to torment the earth with the power granted to each one.

When the first trumpet will sound, one third of the trees and all green grass will be burned up by hail and fire mingled with blood and thrown to the earth (Rev. 8:7).

The second trumpet will sound and a mountain-like fire ball will be thrown into the sea. It will cause the wrath of God to turn a third of the sea to blood, and a third of the living creatures in the sea to die, and a third of the ships in the sea to be destroyed.

The third will make a great star (called wormwood) burning like a torch to fall from heaven. It will poison a third of the rivers and the fresh water. A third of the waters will become wormwood and it will make the water better killing many men.

The fourth will make a third of the sun, moon and stars to be struck, turning a third of them into darkness. A third of the day and night will not shine (Rev. 8:12).

The fifth trumpet will produce an angel who has the key to the bottomless pit. He will open it, and the locusts which will come out from the smoke that will arise from the pit will torment all men who do not have the seal of God on their foreheads (Rev. 9:2–5).

When the sixth trumpet sounds, God will order the release of the previously restrained four angels, now bound at the great river Euphrates. They will be free to harm the earth and the sea, and to kill a third of mankind with fire, smoke and brimstone, and it will be so (Rev. 7:3; 9:14–15).

Then the water of the great river Euphrates will be dried up to prepare the way of the kings from the east (Rev. 16: 10–12). Still the rest of mankind who were not killed will not repent. All those who received the mark of the beast and who worshipped his image will be tormented by the foul and loathsome sores that will come upon them.

The sea will be turned to blood, and every living creature in her will die. The rivers and springs of water will similarly turn to blood (Rev. 16:2–4).

The angel of God shall give power to the sun to scorch men with fire. Still the men will blaspheme the name of God and will not give Him glory.

Then the throne and the kingdom of the beast will be made full of darkness and great pain. Still they will not repent.

An angel of God will come down from heaven to lay hold of Satan. He will bind him for one thousand years and will shut him up in a bottomless pit with a seal set over him (Rev. 20:2–3).

Illustration

Satan restricted from deceiving the nations for one thousand years

Entrance to bottomless pit

Seal over entrance

Bottomless pit

Satan bound and cast into bottomless pit (Rev. 20:31)

Clarification

The scripture is clear regarding the second coming of Christ. So also is the great tribulation as it has been previously examined. The analysis of both which has been done above shows a onetime event in each case. Everyone can understand the scripture differently if the revelation is not from the Holy Spirit. This suggests that reliance on acclaimed authority of old can be misleading if such interpretation is lacking clear biblical support. One can find this debacle in the daily prediction of the second coming of Jesus Christ and the timing of the great tribulation. *Then, one may ask, who are these 'men of God' serving? And how do these efforts help to make nations disciples of Christ?*

All that is important is to start now to be committed to seek the kingdom of God and His righteousness. The day of His coming will be like the visitation of a thief. Therefore there will be no time to do any impromptu change of prevailing choice of belief by anybody. But watch out for the signs which will be made bare before all. Do not let people deceive you about His second coming. It will take all unawares (Lk. 21:8–12).

Apart from watching out for the signs, I believe that the most important concern to man is to start now to believe and abide in Jesus Christ. It is only then that man will have confidence in himself to behold the signs that may come any day, and to receive the Lord Christ Jesus with joy.

As previously explained, this gospel of grace must first be preached throughout the whole earth as a testimony to all nations before the end (Mt. 24:14). The two witnesses of the angel of the thrones of judgment will be instrumental in getting the gospel to all corners of the earth. Chances are that whoever shall brush aside this candid advice might sooner than later contend with the second death, without opportunity to make amend.

Chapter Thirty-Seven

The Purpose of the Second Coming of Christ

1. To end the great tribulation.
2. To execute the first judgment on the allies of Satan, and cage him briefly.
3. To harvest the (first set of) bride to the marriage of the Lamb (rapture).
4. To preside over the first resurrection: the martyrs, beheaded saints etc.
5. To reign for one thousand years on the current earth. (*It will witness the re- building* of the tabernacle of David)
6. To give Satan a second chance, and then cast him into the lake of fire (Chapter 38A).
7. To execute the second resurrection and final judgment (Chapter 38B).
8. To establish the new heaven and earth (New Jerusalem) (Chapter 39)
9. To reign on earth forever (Chapter 39).

Purpose 1 and 2
End of tribulation and the first judgment

The resurrection of Christ from the dead judged and condemned Satan in principle.

Satan's defeat then was a one-time event. It signalled the fall of Babylon, the great harlot which represented the pinnacle of idol worship (Rev. 19:2).

But because the finished work of Jesus was cut short in righteousness, Satan has continued to snare man because of his imperfection (Rom. 9:28). It is this imperfection that will pave way for the great tribulation which was previously examined.

So the second coming of Christ Jesus will herald the completion of the short work which God purposed to do on earth (Rom. 28:22). How?

The short work God did previously resulted in complete holiness and righteousness of the new creation Spirit alone (Eph. 4:24). The second coming of Jesus Christ will result in the investiture of the soul and body with holiness and righteousness.

This suggests that the short time which God gave to Satan will be ripe by then. So the Lord will come to clip his wings (Rev. 12:12). This is the judgment that He will execute on the beast and prophet and his army, and the punishment upon the hardened hearts as examined previously.

Purpose 3
The (first) harvest

The accounts of the scripture clearly show that the second coming of the Lord will mark the end of the great tribulation (Mt. 24:29–31).

The same scripture clearly indicates that the sudden taking up of some saints chosen by God (rapture) will **be tied to the second coming of Jesus Christ.**

His second coming will be after the great tribulation.

This suggests that all the living then will experience the great tribulation before the signs of the time will begin to manifest (Lk. 21:12).

As previously seen, the second coming of Jesus is going to be very sudden, like in the days of Noah when the conceited set their minds on things of earthly life (Mt. 24:37–39).

Therefore now is the time to believe in Jesus to avoid eternal sorrow and torment.

The true bearer of the news of the day of the Lord's coming might emerge today, but only God knows (Mt. 24:42).

Jesus in His first coming finished all that previously kept man away from God. Then all received the command to work out their own salvation until His second coming.

Those who heed the Lord are known as saints. They will rejoice to see the Son of Man descend on a white horse, with great multitudes following Him on white horses (Rev. 19:11, 14). The saints who have previously died in the Lord will rise first and ascend to join the entourage of the Lord in the clouds (1 Thes. 4:14–16).

Then the Lord will send His angels to gather His chosen ones (saints) alive from one end of heaven to the order as previously shown. In addition, the angels will have their lowly bodies transformed to conform to the glorious body of Christ (Phil. 3:21; 1 Cor. 15:51–52).

After the transformation they will be caught up together with the entourage of Christ in the clouds to meet the Lord in the air (1 Thes. 4:17; Mt. 24:30–31). This will be when all those who survived the tribulation will just be recovering from the shock of the distress. The taking-up will equally be sudden. Those left behind will find reason to believe Jesus and to fear God.

Two men walking in field (Lk. 17:36)

One man taken away to the clouds to meet the Lord

One man left behind later

This is the invitation of the first set of people whom God has adjudged faithful to the marriage of the Lamb. On earth it will be a case of the sudden separation of companions from one another (Mt. 24:40–41; Rev. 19:7–9) – the so-called 'rapture'.

All the invitees to the marriage shall remain with the Lord Jesus Christ. They will be where He is in the Father's house or mansion forever (John 14:2–3; 17:24).

Is there anybody who desires to be like the foolish virgins who failed to prepare for the coming of the bridegroom (Mt. 25: 8, 12)?

You can avoid the unpalatable consequences of denying Jesus. Sure you can.

Purpose 4
The judgment of first resurrection by the thrones

This judgment will be for the souls of those martyrs who were beheaded for the sake of the name of Jesus, and the word of God. It will include those beheaded for refusal to both worship the beast or his image, and to receive his mark of 666 on the foreheads or hands. They will be judged by the thrones, which will include the throne of the ancient of days (Dan. 7:9).

Thereafter, they will live and reign with Christ for a thousand years. But the rest of the dead beside these martyrs shall remain dead until the end of the thousand years. *This is the first resurrection (Rev. 20:4–6).*

Meanwhile, there will be those alive who will be left behind on earth. Who will they be?

A remnant of Israel and the one hundred and forty four thousand sealed servants of God will be around. The Christians who will defile the antichrist but will be protected by the grace of God will be there. Gentiles will be there.

Purpose 5
The thousand years' reign of Christ Jesus

The nudge for the one thousand years' reign will be the fullness of the time of the Gentiles. It will be preceded with the fulfilment of the prophecy of the later day rain by Prophet Joe (Joe 2:23).

On the later day rain, Israel will believe that Christ Jesus is the Saviour, as the scripture declared and has been previously shown (Rom. 11:16, 26-27).

Then He will baptise her with the Holy Spirit in the likeness of the Gentiles on the day of Pentecost (Acts 2:4).

This will be on the heel of the ascension to heaven of the two witnesses sent from the throne of judgment as previously shown.

The first resurrection will be predominately Gentiles. This will give credence to the prophecy of Jesus that "the last will be first, and the first last" (Mt. 20:16).

This is to say that the Gentiles were the last to receive the gospel but will become the first to believe in Jesus, and to be resurrected to eternal life.

The rebuilding of the tabernacle of David (Acts 15:16)

This tabernacle is not a physical structure. Rather, it is the manifestation and pursuit of the will of God with zeal, vigour, simplicity and every inherent virtue in man. This will be in the likeness of King David. He was fond of praising and offering thanksgiving to God, feared and trusted in Him, made God his refuge, confessed his sins and quickly repented, and he showed dedication in worship and so on.

All these attributes are made manifest in the book of Psalm and other scriptures which made references to King David.

The one hundred and forty four thousand servants of God that were sealed as previously described will lead the tabernacle of David (Rev. 7:4).

They will be the people to rule in place of the ruler, Christ the Lord, who will oversee all things from the clouds in the form of Spirit. The gospel of the kingdom of God during the thousand years' reign of Christ will get a boost like never before (Is. 4:5–6).

Christ will create a cloud of cover of protection above His dwelling place and above her assemblies and it will include tabernacle of shade and a place of refuge and for shelter from storm and rain (Is. 4:5-6).

God chose Jews as His sons by virtue of His promise to the Patriarchs even before the first coming of Jesus (Is. 27:9; Rom. 11:28–29). The rest of mankind will seek the Lord like never before (Acts 15:17).

This rejuvenated knowledge of God will dominate the reign of the Lord Jesus Christ on earth for the thousand years (Rev. 20:6). All creatures will live in harmony in peace and joy and prosperity.

There will be no strife, no blindness and deafness, no famine or illness and so on (Is.11:6-16; Is. 12; 35: 1-10).

After the thousand years' reign the seal on the bottomless pit will be removed. Then Satan will be released, possibly to give him an opportunity to repent and to demonstrate the just righteousness of God (Rom. 3:26).

There will be men with hardened hearts whom God spared in the post great tribulation killing, that they might repent and be saved (Mt. 24:40). During the period of the reign of Christ the beast and prophet and Satan and their army will not be there to hinder them. So there will be no genuine reason not to repent.

The dead, beside those in the first resurrection, shall not live again until after the thousand years of Christ's reign.

Contrasting post-Noah and post-taking-up of saints

What happened to things left behind on earth after the Noah flood will be different from what will happen to those things that will be left behind after the taking up of selected saints from amongst companions. In the case of Noah, all the things he left behind were wiped out. But in the case of invitation of the select to the marriage of the Lamb, the sudden taking up of men, the things that will be left behind on earth will survive (Lk. 17:34–36).

This suggests that people will be on earth. They will include the one hundred and forty four thousand Israelites that will be sealed before the seventh trumpet will sound. Thus the common thing to both events will be the unexpectedness.

Chapter Thirty-Eight (A)

Mercy Offered to Satan, but He Rebuffed It

Satan's release, his exploit and casting into the lake of fire

After the thousand years' reign of Christ Jesus, Satan will be released from bondage in the bottomless pit. Instead of repenting he will run amok to deceive the nations around the world. In his arsenal will be three unclean spirits like frogs which will come out of his mouth and the mouths of the beast and the prophet (Rev. 16:13).

These spirits of demons, which perform signs, will go out to the kings of the earth and of the whole world which alludes to spirit realm of darkness. They will gather them to war against the Lamb. That will mean war against His disciples, who will be the saints worldwide, and Israel at a place called Armageddon in the Hebrew language (Rev. 16:14, 16).

The king of Gog and Ma-gog, which suggests the present-day prince of Russia, Meshach and Tubal, will gather to attack the Jerusalem that now is (Ezek. 39:1–6). This will be with the intent to trample the holy city, the heritance of God, underfoot (Dan. 8:10), and have the holy temple defiled (Ps. 79:1).

But when they besiege Jerusalem and engage the saints worldwide, fire will come down from God out of heaven and devour them.

Then Satan will be caught and cast into the lake of fire and brimstone, where the beast and false prophet shall have earlier been cast. All will be tormented there forever (Rev. 20:10).

Hailstones will rain on men (Rev. 16: 18–21; Rev. 20:11).

Then God will finally take back His great power, and the dead will be judged. The saints and the prophets will be rewarded and God will destroy those who destroy the earth (Rev. 11:18).

Chapter Thirty-Eight (B)

The Last Day

There will be four major events:

i. The second and final harvest of mankind
ii. Second resurrection and the final judgment by the white throne which will come out from God
iii. The second death
iv. The end of the present heaven and earth

(i).

The great white throne, with the Lord Jesus Christ seated to judge the dead will appear from heaven in the clouds. Jesus will finally reap the last harvest of mankind. In the same period Satan will be finally thrown into the lake of fire. So He will harvest all who died in the Lord during the period of Satan's last attack after his release from the bottomless pit (Rev. 14:13).

Additionally He will harvest to Himself all the living who abided in Him to the end (Mt. 13:24, 30b) to rest for their labor (Rev. 14:14-16).

Those who denied Jesus will be reaped separately as tares (Mt. 13:25, 30a) and then thrown into the lake of fire where Satan will be (Rev. 14:17-20).

The demise of Satan will signal the end of the current heaven and earth which were prisons for the disobedient as shown previously in Chapter 1.

(ii)

All the dead besides those who were of the first resurrection will be raised from the dead. They will all be judged in accordance with their works and what were written in either the book of life or the book (Rev. 20:12).

The 'book of life' will be the record of names of obedient servants and the 'book' will be the record of names of the disobedient creation.

The sea and Death and Hades are the abode of alienated spirit from the light of God. They will hand over the dead in them. Then they will be judged according to the works of the individual.

Anyone whose name is not found in the book of life will be cast into the lake of fire. Finally Hades and Death will be the last to be cast into the lake of fire.

The books will contain assessment standards for: words spoken; way of life; things done in secret; works done in the body of Christ; conscience and law of Moses.

This suggests that both the born again and unbeliever will be examined.

(iii).

The demise of Satan will signal the end of the current heaven and earth. They have respectively been the prison for the spirit and human who disobeyed God, as shown previously in Chapter 1

The final cast of Satan and the rest into the lake of fire is the second death, which is a biblical term for an everlasting separation from God (Rev. 20:13–15).

(iv).

At last, the present earth and heaven will flee away infinitely from the face of the Lord when the throne of judgment shall emerge from God (2 Pet. 3:7; Rev. 20:11).

Illustration of the end of the present heaven and earth (Rev. 20:11)

In the end, the air shall receive a bowl of the anger of God (Rev. 16:17).

Great earthquake and strange happening will hit the earth like have never happened before and the cities of the nations of the world will fall. The great Babylon, the credo and seat of all abominations, will receive the fierceness of the anger of God.

Every island will flee away infinitely and mountains will vanish as depicted in the next page.

Model of end of present heaven and earth (Dan. 2:35a, Rev. 20:11)

Great white throne emerging (Rev. 20:11)

The present heaven and earth will flee away infinitely from the face of the Lord (Rev. 16:20). All the elements on terrestrial earth and visible heaven of firmament will melt by fervent heart (2 Peter. 3:10).

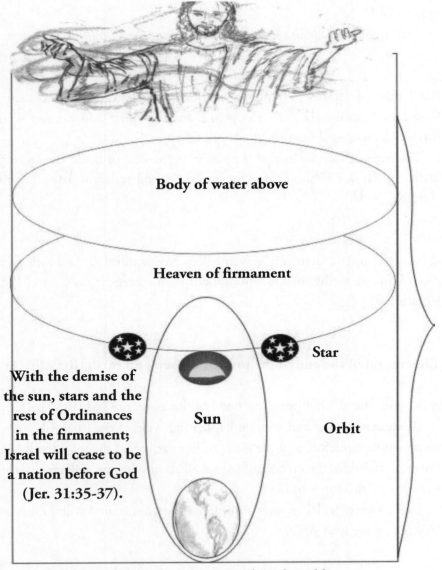

Body of water above

Heaven of firmament

Star

With the demise of the sun, stars and the rest of Ordinances in the firmament; Israel will cease to be a nation before God (Jer. 31:35-37).

Sun

Orbit

The present time based terrestrial earth and heaven

Chapter Thirty-Nine

Model of the New Heaven and Earth

The passing away of the current heaven and earth will hasten the coming of the day of God (2 Pet. 3:12). It will usher in the new heaven and new earth. In both, only righteousness will dwell in fulfilment of the promise of God (Is. 65:17; Rev. 21:1).

The seventh angel of the seventh seal shall proclaim the coming of the new heaven and new earth. Christ and God will dwell there and reign forever (Rev. 11:15).

Finally the new heaven and new earth will emerge out of heaven from God.

The holy city, which is the prophesied New Jerusalem, will also come down out of heaven. She will be adorned with strength and beautiful garments, prepared like a bride for her husband (Is. 52:1), who will be the Lord Jesus Christ (2 Cor. 11:2).

There will be no more death nor sorrow, nor any other afflictions known and unknown now and forever (Rev. 21:4). All things shall become new, and they will be the inheritance for the inhabitants, all of who shall have overcome death (Rev. 21:7).

The Lord God and the Lamb will be the temple. As shown in Chapter 1, God is the ultimate source of light. Therefore in the new heaven and earth there will be no other source of light. The glory of God will prevail and the Lamb shall be the light, and there will be no night (Rev. 22–23).

Our Lord Jesus Christ shall reign forever in her.

Model of emerging new heaven and new earth (Dan. 2:35b, Rev. 21:1)

The Great white thrones and God was seated (Dan. 7:9).

The holy Jerusalem coming down
out of heaven from God
(Rev. 21:10).

Twelve gates of the four-sided city, with three gates on each
four sides (Rev. 21:12-13) and one angel beside each gate (Rev.
21:12–13).

The New Jerusalem is also known as the great city of the new earth. In outline, the city will be square in length and width and height. Its total measure will be roughly 1,380 miles (Rev. 21:12, 16).

Each side of the city shall have three gates. The total number of gates shall be twelve, and every gate shall be of a different pearl. Every gate shall have one name of the twelve tribes of Israel written on it (Ezek. 48:31–34).

The city will have high walls (Rev. 21:12). The walls of the great city shall be twelve storeys high, and each foundation shall be adorned with precious stones of different kinds. Each shall similarly bear the name of one of the apostles of the Lamb (Rev. 21:14, 19–20).

The complex will be in the likeness of the foundation of the gospel of grace, whose foundation Apostle Paul laid, with Jesus as the chief cornerstone (1 Cor. 3:10–11). The street will be paved with pure gold in the likeness of transparent glass (Rev. 21:21).

There will be a pure river of the water of life. On each side of the river and in the middle of the street there shall at each place be the tree of life. The tree will bear twelve fruits and shall yield its fruit every month, and its leaves shall be for healing the nations (Rev. 22:2).

This is the earth to which God alluded when He promised Abraham that he will be heir of the earth (Rom. 4:13), and when He said to him: *And in you all the families of the earth shall be blessed* (Gen. 12:3b).

All the families in this earth will indeed be blessed. *That the tree of life will be there shows that the Garden of Eden was in the celestial earth shown in Chapter 1.*

Also, it is the earth where all the virtues which Jesus taught the multitudes as the beatitudes in His Sermon on the Mount will fully manifest in all men (Mt. 5:3–14). So all will have pure hearts and shall see the face of God, and His name shall be on their foreheads (Rev. 22:4).

This is the kingdom of heaven which Jesus eloquently preached to man (Mt. 13:45). Only the just whose names are written in the Lamb's book of life will enter the kingdom (Mt. 25:32).

All the saved souls will be arrayed in white robes and serve God forever (Rev. 7:15). The dwelling place of God (tabernacle) shall be with these saved men.

The soul of God will not detest men, but will dwell with them as His people and their God (Rev. 21:3).

In the New Jerusalem all things will be new and free to all the inhabitants. It will be a place to live forever in joy, peace, gladness and righteousness without any traces of the evil of the present earth (Is. 25:8). Indeed, there shall be no evil in the new heaven and earth and there shall be no sun nor moon, nor sea.

The Lord God Almighty and the Lamb shall be everything good that will be required in the kingdom (Rev. 21:23). All men shall walk in the way of the Lord, which shall be without shadow of turning, or darkness or lie (Rev. 21:25).

In retrospect the light of the likeness of night in the new world will be liken to the moon at night increased to the light of the sun in the present world.

The light of the likeness of the day in the new world will be liken to the light of the sun increased sevenfold, as the light of seven days in the present world (Is. 30:26).